Lynn Ann Majidimehr

Flower Show Quilts

Stunning Appliqué on a Patchwork Canvas

Martingale®
& COMPANY

Flower Show Quilts:
Stunning Appliqué on a Patchwork Canvas
© 2010 by Lynn Ann Majidimehr

That Patchwork Place® is an imprint
of Martingale & Company®.

Martingale & Company
19021 120th Ave. NE, Suite 102
Bothell, WA 98011 USA
www.martingale-pub.com

Printed in China

15 14 13 12 11 10   8 7 6 5 4 3 2 1

Library of Congress Cataloging-in-Publication
Data is available upon request.

ISBN: 978-1-56477-934-2

Mission Statement

*Dedicated to providing quality products
and service to inspire creativity.*

Credits

President & CEO ✳ Tom Wierzbicki

Editor in Chief ✳ Mary V. Green

Managing Editor ✳ Tina Cook

Developmental Editor ✳ Karen Costello Soltys

Technical Editor ✳ Nancy Mahoney

Copy Editor ✳ Marcy Heffernan

Design Director ✳ Stan Green

Production Manager ✳ Regina Girard

Illustrator ✳ Laurel Strand

Cover & Text Designer ✳ Regina Girard

Photographer ✳ Brent Kane

Dedication

To my wonderful husband and family, thank you for giving me the time to make quilts, write, and take care of business, even when it meant that there was less time for other things. Without your help and support it would have been impossible to write this book.

Contents

The Projects

Introduction

I love variety! Flowers are one subject I keep coming back to because they're so beautiful and come in so many different sizes, shapes, and colors. My mother had a huge collection of orchids, and although I've also had some, hers always grew larger and were more beautiful. I remember a beautiful passionflower vine that was in my grandparents' yard when I was little, and the gardenia bushes that my mom and aunt had. Flowers can be symbols for many things and are given for many reasons, but they're always beautiful. I've filled this book with an assortment of projects, from wall quilts to lap-sized quilts, and even something for adorning your table. My hope is that you'll choose a project and make it fit you, your home, or whomever you make it for.

Quiltmaking Basics

There are many different methods to make a quilt, and everyone has her preferences—sometimes because it's how she was taught from the beginning, sometimes it's a technique for speed or accuracy, and sometimes it's just because she's always done it that way. I've included the methods I used to create the quilts in this book so you can use the techniques that I did.

Use a ¼" seam allowance for all seams unless indicated otherwise. When rotary cutting, a standard ¼" seam allowance is included in the measurements. Templates for appliqué patterns do not include a seam allowance.

Sewing Supplies

Sewing machine. A good working machine is a joy to use. A machine that isn't working properly can be frustrating and make it difficult to attain the desired results. These projects don't require a fancy sewing machine; all you need is to be able to stitch forward and backward, zigzag, and sew using an accurate ¼" seam allowance. You'll need to be able to drop the feed dogs if you want to do free-motion quilting, and a walking foot is helpful for in-the-ditch quilting and for attaching binding.

Sewing-machine needles. The type and size of needles to use will depend on your chosen threads—you don't need all of these needles, just the type required for the thread you're using. These are my current preferences.

✳ Sharp or Jeans needles—80/12. I use them for piecing, and occasionally for quilting too.

✳ Metallic needles—80/12. Specifically made for handling metallic thread without shredding it, they aren't as sharp as topstitching needles. Therefore, you may need to use a topstitching needle on tightly woven fabrics, such as batiks. Some threads work best with either metallic or topstitching needles.

✳ Sharp or Jeans needles—70/10. Use them for invisible appliqué and for machine beading (if your needle fits loosely through your bead); otherwise, use a 60/8 (Sharp or Universal) needle when using thin or transparent thread.

✳ Quilting needles—Klasse 80/12 or Schmetz 75/11. These are strong and sharp, made for machine quilting through the layers of a quilt using standard 50-weight sewing thread.

✳ Topstitching needles—80/12, 90/14, or 100/16. The large eye and sharp point make them suitable for 30- and 40-weight threads (I've used size 110/18 for really heavy thread). If I could purchase only one type of needle for machine quilting, it would be a Topstitching 80/12 (although a 90/14 would run a close second) because of the threads I like to use. If you're machine quilting batik fabrics, try a smaller needle first, and then change to a larger needle if needed.

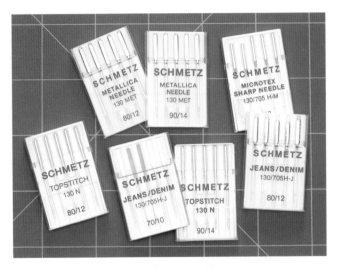

Sewing-machine needles come in a variety of types and sizes.

Presser feet. You'll need a ¼" presser foot for piecing; an open-toe, embroidery foot for machine appliqué; and a darning or free-motion foot for quilting. A walking foot is helpful for stitch-in-the-ditch quilting and applying binding.

Free-motion quilting foot

Other supplies. You probably already have most of these items on hand.

* Regular or small embroidery scissors for clipping threads.

* Hand-sewing and beading needles. I prefer size 10 milliner's or appliqué needles.

* Rotary cutter, acrylic rulers, and cutting mat. While I find it useful to have a collection of different sizes, 8½" x 24" and 8½" x 12" rulers are the ones I reach for regularly.

* Straight pins for patchwork and #1 safety pins for pin basting.

* Sewing thread to match or blend with fabric for piecing and hand sewing, and quilting thread to match or coordinate with fabric for quilting. My favorite thread for quilting is Superior Threads Rainbows thread, because I love the colors that are available, but I also use many other threads. I almost always use Superior Threads Bottom Line thread in the bobbin, because it's thinner, virtually trouble free, and I can usually find a color that will blend with my quilt back.

* Extension table for your machine (many of these are clear acrylic) is essential for control when machine quilting if your sewing machine sits on top of a table.

* Quilting discs or gloves will help you control your quilt when free-motion quilting.

* Camera, reducing glass, or door peephole is helpful for looking at your quilt as if from a distance.

* Design wall for laying out the pieces for your block or quilt top to preview the colors before sewing them together and to make sure the blocks (or quilt top) are assembled correctly. It's better to waste a little fabric cutting new pieces than to make all the blocks or sew the whole quilt top together, and then not like it. For years I worked on the floor, and I still do when my project is too large for my design wall.

Selecting Your Fabrics

I believe in making projects with fabrics you love, so if the project is shown in Asian prints and you love batiks or hand-dyed fabrics, go ahead and make it in the fabrics that please you. Subtle quilts can also be made in bright colors with black or dark backgrounds for a knock-your-socks-off bold look. You can also do the reverse; re-create a bold-colored quilt in subtle tone-on-tone fabrics or watercolor batiks, for a totally different look to complement a living space. What really matters is that you use fabrics that you love to get the look that will make you happy. If you love a design but not the fabric, take a look around you and use fabrics and colors that appeal to you or that will work with your surroundings.

When choosing fabrics, try to stack the bolts or fabric pieces so that you're able to see the proportional sizes of each one. You should be able to see a larger amount of the main fabric, or large borders, and just the bolt edges or folded fat quarters of the other fabrics that will be used for smaller parts of a block or for appliqué. This will help you see how the fabrics fit together, or if one stands out and screams "look at me" instead of blending with the other fabrics.

Most of the flowers and plants in my quilts are similar in color to those found in nature, but I often adapt the colors of a quilt to suit a particular room. Sometimes I will choose the appliqué fabrics, assemble the appliqué, and then audition fabrics for the pieced background. Other times I start with a gorgeous piece of fabric that will be used as a border or background for my quilt, and then choose the other colors or coordinates to find what looks best with it.

Fabric selection for "Jeweled Orchids" (page 34)

Fabric selection for "Pink Dahlias" (page 78)

I made the "Summer Floral Table Runner" on page 41 in three different color combinations so you can see what a difference the choice of fabric can make.

Changing fabric color or style can dramatically change the look of a quilt.

Fabric Preparation

To avoid surprises later, it's always best to prewash and iron your fabrics before cutting. I realize that this isn't always possible, especially when you're in a class at a quilt shop and need to use fabric that you've just purchased. If this is the case, I recommend that the first time you wash a quilt, you use a dye-catching product or color-catcher sheet to try and control any loose dye from spoiling your beautiful work.

Foundation Piecing

When I first tried foundation piecing, I didn't like picking out all the paper, and so I sometimes used muslin foundations that became part of the quilt. In the past few years I tried using wash-away foundations, and then I learned how to use freezer paper as a foundation. The freezer-paper method is now my favorite method.

1. Copy or trace the foundation pattern onto the dull side of the freezer paper. Cut out the freezer-paper foundation on the dark solid line around the foundation's outer edges.

2. Press the shiny side of the freezer-paper foundation onto the wrong side of fabric 1, making sure the fabric covers section 1 and extends at least ¼" beyond all seam lines. (It doesn't need to be the same shape as the section, since it will be trimmed later.) If you can't see the fabric through the foundation, hold the pieces up to a light source so you can position the fabric correctly.

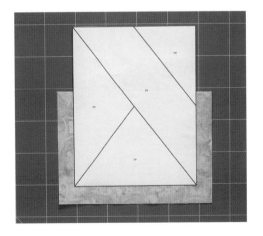

3. With the marked side of the foundation facing you, place an index card or postcard on the line between sections 1 and 2 and fold the foundation and fabric over the card. Make a crease along the line, and then unfold the fabric *only*.

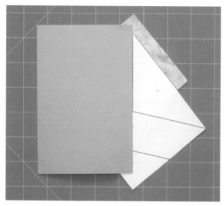

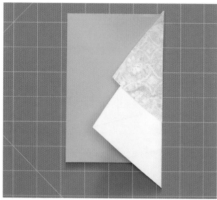

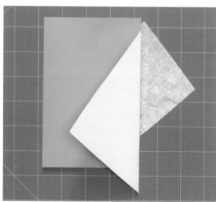

4. Place fabric 2 on your table, right side facing up. Now place your foundation and fabric 1 on top, making sure that the fabric completely covers section 2 and extends a generous ¼" beyond all seam lines. Stitching on the fabrics only, sew as closely as you can to the folded edge of the freezer paper without sewing on the paper. Start stitching

at least ¼" before the seam line and stop stitching at least ¼" beyond.

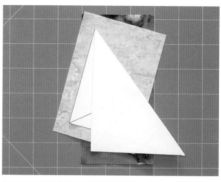

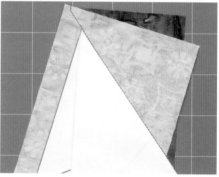

5. Using an Add-A-Quarter ruler or a regular rotary ruler, place the ruler along the folded edge of the paper and trim the seam allowances to ¼". Unfold the freezer paper; on the right side of the fabrics, press the seam allowances toward fabric 2. *Do not touch the iron to the shiny side of the paper.*

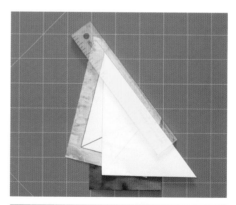

6. In the same manner, place the card between sections 2 and 3. Fold the foundation and fabrics along the seam line, and then unfold the *fabrics only.* With right sides together, place the foundation on fabric 3, making sure the fabric covers section 3 and extends a generous ¼" beyond all seam lines. Stitch along the paper's folded edge, trim the seam allowances to ¼", and then press them toward fabric 3.

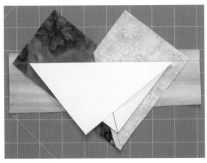

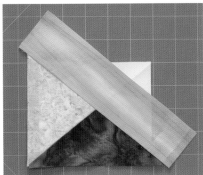

7. Continue in the same manner to add fabric 4. Press the completed block on the right side.

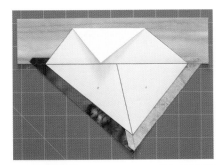

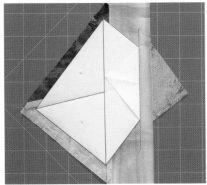

8. With the freezer-paper foundation facing you, use your rotary cutter to trim the fabrics ¼" from the foundation on all sides. Do not remove the paper yet. Remove the paper after you join the blocks to other blocks or fabric so that the edges will be stabilized.

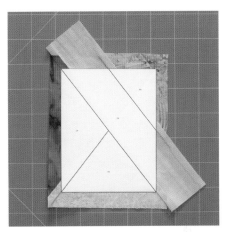

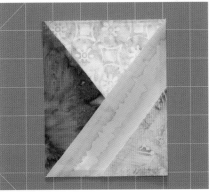

Appliqué

Some designs in this book have appliqués that need to be attached before the border is added; for other designs the border is added, and then appliqués are attached. And in one design, the appliqués will be partially attached before the border is joined, and then finished afterward. So pay close attention to the assembly order in each project.

Using Templates

If you prefer tracing around a template when the same shape is used many times in a design, you may want to make a reusable plastic template. Use a permanent marker to trace the design onto the template plastic. Do not add a seam allowance. Use utility scissors to cut out the template, cutting exactly on the line. Then you can quickly trace the design as many times as you need. Plastic templates work particularly well for some leaves, smaller flowers, and flower petals.

Fusible Appliqué

Please read, understand, and follow the manufacturer's instructions that come with your fusible web, since there are many different products available today. Some products, like paper-backed fusible web, require you to reverse the pattern, and depending on your iron, you may need to use a different temperature than you normally use for piecing.

The fused projects in this book were made using Mistyfuse and the instructions below. Mistyfuse is a paperless, ultra-fine fusible web, so the patterns don't need to be reversed—except for designs that also use mirror-image pieces, like a leaf and reversed leaf. I like this product, because I can layer the appliqués without adding bulk or stiffness to my design. Since it's very lightweight, I don't mind having this fusible web underneath the entire appliqué shape, and it's easier for me to work with some appliqué shapes using this method. If the appliqué shape is large, I might choose a different method, such as the "Freezer-Paper, Glue-Basted Appliqué" technique on page 13, or a combination of both methods, as I did for "Jeweled Orchids" on page 34. (To reduce waste, when cutting shapes from the fused fabrics, I cut the larger pieces first, and then cut the smaller pieces from the leftover fabric.)

1. Trace the required number of appliqué shapes onto the dull side of freezer paper, grouping shapes that will be cut from the same fabric and adding a ¼" seam allowance where one shape needs to go underneath its neighbor. Cut the shapes apart, grouping like pieces together in one large piece that will be cut from the same fabric.

2. Using a dry iron, press the shiny side of the freezer paper to the right side of your fabric and cut out the single unit, leaving about ½" all around.

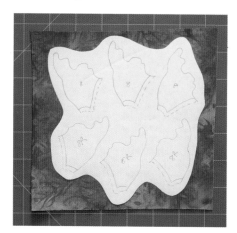

Freezer-paper shapes ironed to right side of fabric

3. Use a piece of parchment paper that is larger than the freezer-paper/fabric shape to cover your ironing surface. Cut a second piece of parchment paper about the same size and set it aside.

Parchment Paper

Parchment paper has a silicone coating that makes the surface of the paper nonstick. I recommend using Reynolds brand, which is available in the kitchen aisle at most grocery stores.

4. Place Mistyfuse on the parchment paper; you'll need enough to cover your freezer-paper/fabric shape. (If the shape is larger than the parchment paper, you may need to apply the fusible web in sections.) Place the fabric side of the freezer-paper/fabric shape on top of the Mistyfuse and trim away any excess fusible web.

5. Cover the freezer-paper/fabric shape with the second piece of parchment paper and press to adhere the fusible web to the fabric. If necessary, turn the pieces over and press again from the other side, making sure the parchment paper covers the fusible web.

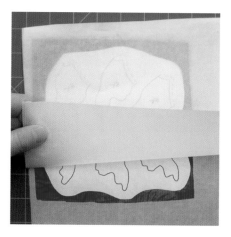

Freezer-paper/fabric shape and fusible web sandwiched between parchment paper

6. Cut out the appliqué shapes on the marked lines, leaving the freezer-paper attached for now.

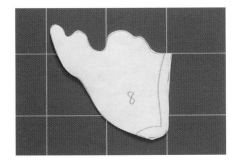

Appliqué cut out with freezer-paper attached

7. Enlarging the pattern if needed, trace the pattern from the book onto a piece of paper to make a placement guide. Cover the placement guide with a piece of parchment paper and use the pattern to position the pieces as you build your appliqué shape. For more complex appliqué units, I prefer to assemble the shapes from the center outward using the tip of the iron to tack the center of each piece in place, and then tucking the other pieces underneath as needed. Once all of the pieces are assembled, cover them with parchment paper and press the entire shape.

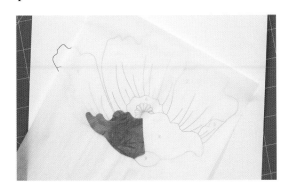

First appliqué piece on parchment paper with placement guide visible below

Adding appliqué pieces

Sliding piece underneath adjacent shape

Completed appliqué shape

8. Remove the assembled appliqué shape from the parchment paper. Position the shape *adhesive side down* on the right side of the background fabric (or quilt top) as described in the instructions for the project you're making. Cover the shape with parchment paper and press. (If the appliqués extend into the border, fuse the pieces to within about 1" of the quilt center's outer edges only.)

9. Generally, I prefer to finish most appliqué edges when I'm quilting my quilt, either by quilting close to the raw edges and leaving them raw, or for some shapes, such as leaves, I use a free-motion zigzag stitch to quilt and cover the shape at the same time, adding texture to the edges. However, if you wish to finish the raw edges before layering your quilt, you can use a decorative machine stitch, such as zigzag or satin stitch.

Freezer-Paper, Glue-Basted Appliqué

These appliqués are assembled from the bottom up, and then machine appliquéd to adjoining pieces, a block, or the quilt top.

1. Begin by tracing the templates from your pattern onto the dull side of your freezer paper with a permanent marker. (*Don't* add a space between the pieces, as they need to be one piece, just like the

pattern.) Using a colored pencil or marker, add reference marks crossing the pattern lines to help you put the appliqués together again. Assign a letter to each of your traced units and add it to the number on the individual pieces. This will enable you to put flower A together separately from flower B, and allow for any little differences in your tracings. Once this is done, cut the freezer-paper templates apart, cutting directly on the traced lines.

Pattern traced onto freezer paper, with red reference marks and letters and numbers

2. Press the freezer-paper templates to the *right side* of your fabric. Cut out the fabric shapes, adding ¼" all around for seam allowances. Clip inner curves, stopping a couple threads before reaching the template.

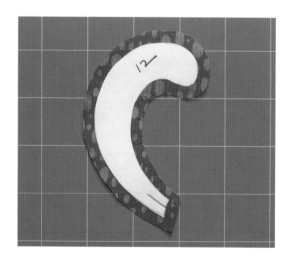

Seam allowance added to fabric shape and inner curves clipped

3. On the *wrong side,* use a glue stick to apply glue to the fabric near the edge of the pattern. (Use a light hand when applying the glue; too much glue can make the pieces difficult to work with.) Gently fold the seam allowance to the wrong side until you see the edge of the freezer-paper, and then press the seam allowance down into the glue. Do not apply glue to an edge that will lie underneath another piece, since that edge will not be turned under. Once you're satisfied with the glue-basted seam allowance, wipe off any excess glue. Turn the piece over so the wrong side is facing down on a piece of parchment paper. Press to set the folded edge completely. Repeat with the rest of the appliqués.

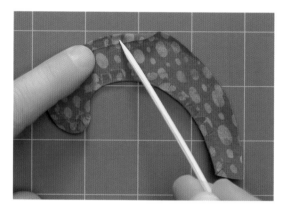

Glue-basted seam allowance

4. Once all of the appliqué pieces are prepared, apply glue to any seam allowance that will lie underneath a neighboring piece, referring to the pattern as needed. Place the neighboring piece on top of the seam allowance, aligning the reference marks. Finger-press in place, and then iron to dry the glue, making it more permanent.

Appliqué pieces glue basted to adjoining pieces

5. Continue combining the pieces until the appliqué unit is complete; press. The freezer paper may be removed now, or after the unit has been glue basted to the block or quilt top.

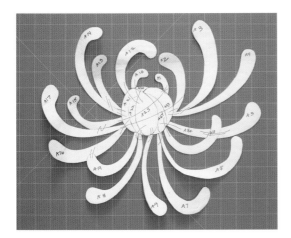

Assembled appliqué unit with freezer paper attached

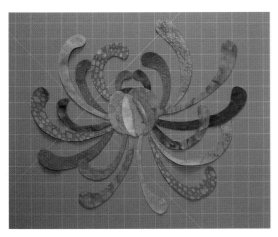

Assembled appliqué unit with freezer paper removed

6. Referring to the photo for the project you're making, glue baste the appliqués in place on the block or quilt top.

7. Hand or machine appliqué the pieces in place. For machine appliqué, you can use a blind hem stitch, sewing along the folded edge of a piece so that the straight stitches are in the background fabric, very close to the folded edge, and the swing stitch just catches a couple threads of the folded edge. If you use a narrow zigzag stitch, sew along the folded edge of a piece so that the needle catches a couple threads on the appliqué and is very close to the folded edge as it enters the background fabric.

Assembling the Quilt Top

I like to keep things interesting, so my quilts don't always fit into a traditional setting layout. Occasionally sections need to be assembled, and then sewn together, sort of like piecing a block. Actually, a couple of the quilt backgrounds really are one single block! If you take the time to read the instructions, look at the assembly diagrams, and lay out the quilt blocks or sections before starting to sew them together, they'll go together quickly and easily.

Borders with Mitered Corners

1. Measure the length and width of the quilt in at least three places. Using the average measurement, add two times the width of the border, and then add 4" to 5" to give yourself some leeway. Cut border strips to the determined lengths.

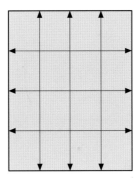

2. Mark the center of the quilt edges on all sides and mark the center of each border.

3. Match the centers of the quilt and borders; stitch the borders to opposite sides of the quilt top, beginning and ending ¼" from the corners of the quilt. The borders will be longer than the quilt. Do not trim.

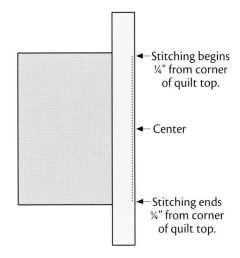

Stitching begins ¼" from corner of quilt top.

Center

Stitching ends ¼" from corner of quilt top.

4. Repeat with the two remaining borders, again starting and stopping ¼" from the edge of the quilt.

5. Place one corner of the quilt top right side up on your ironing board and smooth the border strips away from the quilt center, letting the loose corners overlap as shown.

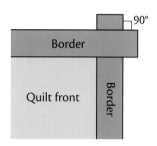

6. Fold the top border up and under at a 45° angle, so that the border strips are directly on top of each other, right sides together. Press a crease along the folded edge and pin in place.

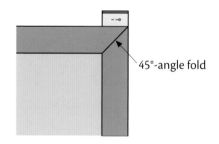

45°-angle fold

7. Unfold the creased border and fold the quilt diagonally, right sides together, and then pin on the creased line. (If the creased line is difficult to see you can mark it with a chalk line, usually pins are all I need to see the line.) Beginning at the inside edge of the quilt, stitch on the creased line, removing the pins as you come to them (do not sew over your pins).

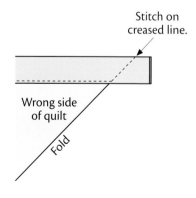

Stitch on creased line.

Wrong side of quilt

Fold

8. Trim away the excess border fabric, leaving a ¼" seam allowance. Press the seam allowances open. Repeat with the remaining corners.

Trim mitered seams and press open.

Layering and Basting

My preferred basting method is pin basting. I use safety pins to hold the layers together, removing them as I'm quilting. The pins are placed about 3" to 4" apart. On larger quilts, the pins are placed closer together because the quilt will be handled more in the quilting process, and there is more chance of the layers shifting.

Begin by laying the quilt back wrong side up on the floor or a table. Use masking tape to anchor the edges. Lay the batting over the quilt back, smoothing out any wrinkles. If I plan to cut the hanging sleeve from the same piece of fabric, I place the batting along one side or in a corner of the backing to reserve as much fabric as possible for the sleeve, while still allowing at least 1" to 2" of backing on all sides. Lay the quilt top, right side up, over the backing, smoothing out any wrinkles. Pin baste the layers together.

Machine Quilting

As far as I'm concerned, quilting is part of making a quilt, probably because when my aunt taught me to quilt, it was just part of the process. I thought you might like to know how I set up my machine and some of my favorite quilting motifs that you can use to finish your quilts.

Machine Setup

* Lower or cover the feed dogs

* Attach a free-motion quilting or darning foot

* Insert a new needle that is the right type for your thread and fabric

Adjust the Height!

One thing that's frequently overlooked—but is important and can't be stressed enough—is the height of your machine when compared to you! It really follows the same principle as typing—when you put your hands on either side of the machine's presser foot, your elbows should be at about a 90° angle. If your hands are higher than your elbows, not only will it be hard on your arms and shoulders, but it will be harder to move the quilt. If you're tensing up your shoulders, you won't be able to quilt very well, or for very long.

Marking Your Design

I prefer not to mark my quilt at all, but I will mark a more complicated part of a design or mark guidelines to help keep the design in shape. For example, when quilting a feather circle, I would only mark three circles: one would be the inside boundary, one the outside boundary, and the other circle would be in between, where the vein of the feather needs to be. You can make your own quilting stencil using transparency film, which is available at most office-supply stores. Use a permanent marker to trace the design onto the transparency, or you can print a design from your computer (make sure you're using the proper type of transparency for your printer). Without threading your sewing machine, stitch on the lines to perforate the design. Use a pouncing powder or rub chalk through the holes to transfer the design onto your quilt.

Checking the Thread Tension

Free-motion quilt, or doodle, as best you can in the shape of a wiggly line, loops (think lowercase e), or a zigzag shape. If the bobbin thread is showing on the top of your quilt, you'll need to loosen the upper tension. If the upper thread is showing on the bottom, you need to tighten the upper tension. Test and adjust until you're happy with the stitching.

Things to Remember

✳ Your machine should always be going faster than your hands are moving the quilt; otherwise, you risk breaking the needle by pulling it with the quilt and having it hit the needle plate.

✳ Keep the bulk of the quilt to the left of the needle and make sure that the area you'll be working on can move freely.

✳ Always thread the machine with the foot in the up position and lower the foot to thread the needle.

✳ Always pull the bobbin thread tail to the top and hold both threads before starting to quilt.

✳ When you need to rearrange the quilt or reposition your hands, stop with the needle in the down position; this keeps the quilt from moving out of place.

✳ Before stitching a design that is new to you, pretend you're quilting and move the quilt as you would to stitch the design. This lets you practice without wasting anything.

✳ When possible, try to stop and start in less-noticeable areas, such as in the ditch between patches. (Sometimes where you stop can't be helped, especially when the thread breaks, the bobbin runs out, or you'd like a line to just start or stop, like in the center of a swirl.)

✳ There are two methods for beginning and ending a line of stitching. My preferred method is to sew tiny stitches for a short distance to begin and end my stitching. Another method is to bury thread tails. (I use this method if I make a quilt specifically to enter in a show, because some judges feel it demonstrates an attention to detail and good-quality work.) To bury the thread tails, knot the thread tails, and then use a needle to pull them into the batting without catching the quilt top or backing.

✳ If the thread breaks or you run out, you can trim the tails closely, and then start again by overlapping the first few stitches with the last few that were made before the thread broke, splitting the previous stitches.

✳ If your machine has a speed control, try setting it on a medium to slow speed so that you can put your foot all the way down on the pedal and have the machine run at a steady speed.

Quilting Designs

In this section, you'll find some of the quilting designs I used on my quilts to give you some ideas for quilting your quilts. We'll start with a basic free-motion stipple and progress to more complex designs.

Stippling or Meandering

Stippling is a close, puzzle-like design, and most of the time I prefer not to cross the threads, although, other times I'll cross the stitching here and there just for fun. Meandering can be a larger version of stippling, or it can include loops, hearts, stars, and other shapes. I've even put simplified butterflies in my meandering!

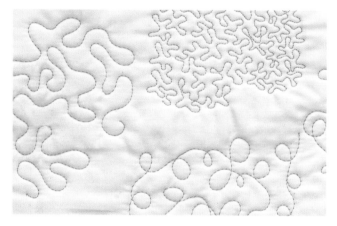

Stipple and meandering quilting

Swirls

Swirls are made by stitching into the center and back out again, and they'll look their best if you make a smooth curve as you exit one swirl and enter the next one. The center of a swirl can be pointed or curved, but I try to make all the swirls in a project with the same type of center.

Swirl quilting design

Triangles or Angled Lines

When I was learning machine quilting, triangles were one of the most challenging designs I learned. I only made friends with this design after deciding to use it in a large area of a quilt. Start by quilting in the shape of a "V" or "W;" change direction and start making a triangle. Instead of completing the triangle, change the direction of the stitched line before it reaches the starting point, or extend it beyond the starting point. Then change direction again and begin a new triangle, "V," or "W" shape, continuing in the same manner until the area is filled.

Triangular or zigzag quilting

Grapes or Stones

To make grapes or stones, start by making circles. You'll have less backtracking (stitching over previous stitching) if you stitch in a modified figure eight, and then sew over the previous stitching when you need to change direction. When I miss quilting an area, I work my way back into it by following my quilting trail. To go back out and continue, I try to find another path so as not to have too much thread buildup, which would make it more obvious.

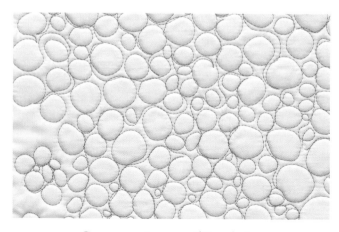

Grapes or stones quilting design

Teardrops or Nested Quilting

To make a teardrop, begin at the base of the teardrop and stitch away from the starting point; then curve out around and back. Repeat, stitching around the shape two more times, each time making a larger teardrop in the same shape as the first. To continue, start another teardrop or loop. Depending on the look you want, the loop can stop where it touches a previously stitched teardrop, or you can create a line of stitched loops. This is where you need to start thinking about direction and where you're going. If you do happen to go in the wrong direction, you can either backtrack over previous stitching, or make another loop to get you headed back in the right direction. This method can be used to quilt other nested shapes as shown below.

Nested quilting designs

Leaf and Vine Shapes

Simple leaves attached to a stem can make a simple branch. Start at the bottom of the branch and make a curvy stem up to where the top leaf will be. Stitch around the top leaf, and then head back down the stem, making pairs of leaves as you go. Stitch on one side first, and then cross the stem and make another leaf on the opposite side. Continue to the base of the stem. On one branch (above right) a row of echo quilting was added inside the leaf, and on the branch in the upper-right corner a partial center vein was added to each leaf.

Leaf and vine quilting

Flowers

You can create flowers by combining swirls, grapes, and teardrops. Add more shapes and come up with your own quilting designs.

Quilted flower designs

Feathers

The feathers shown on page 20 are stitched from different directions: bottom to top, top to bottom, and in the last one the vein was stitched first. Try all three and see which one works best for you.

Bottom-to-top feather (shown on left): This feather begins at the top of the vein. Stitch a slightly curved line to make a vein; when you reach the bottom, pause. Then create an elongated half heart or teardrop shape, going out away from the vein, up around, and back to the vein. Backtrack or stitch close to the previous stitching going away from the vein, and then up, around, and back toward the vein again. Repeat, making gradually smaller teardrops as you near the top. Make a teardrop shape at the top. Head back down the other side of the vein, stitching teardrops about ⅛" from the vein, starting with small teardrops and gradually increasing the size. When you reach the bottom, sew another line of stitching between the teardrops, working your way back up to the top to complete the vein. If you're using stipple stitching to fill in between feathers, you can stipple stitch to get from one feather to where you want to start another.

Top-to-bottom feather (shown in center): This feather begins at the bottom of the vein. Stitch a slightly curved line to make a vein; when you reach the top, make a teardrop shape. Starting with small teardrops and gradually increasing the size, create teardrops on one side of the vein, working back down to the bottom. After one side is completed, stitch the other side of the vein, working your way back to the top of the feather, starting with small teardrops and gradually increasing the size.

Vein-first feather (shown on right): Starting at the bottom of the vein, stitch a slightly curved line to the top of the feather and then back down, leaving a space between the rows of stitching to create the vein. Next stitch teardrops on one side, working from the bottom to the top, starting with large teardrops and gradually deceasing the size. Then work from the top down on the other side, only touching or coming close to the center vein.

Clusters of feathers: When quilting a cluster of feathers, I usually begin by marking where the vein lines will be, without respect to dimension. Once I've determined the overall shape by the vein, I decide on a stitching order. The order in which the feathers are stitched will make one feather come to the front of the cluster and move another to the middle or back. (The first feather that's stitched is the one that appears to come to the front.) The larger, more elaborate feathers just require more planning, and of course when quilting them, you'll be moving the quilt top a further distance as you stitch each one.

Cluster of feathers

Embroidery

I like to use simple hand-embroidery stitches and beads to add details that are too small to appliqué easily, as well as to jazz up a quilt.

Outline or Stem Stitch

An outline or stem stitch are the same stitch; the only difference between the two is the placement of the working thread. For the outline stitch, the working thread is held above the needle. For the stem stitch, hold the thread below the needle as the stitch is worked. I use the names (and stitches) interchangeably, but I test the thread that I'm using with the stitch, as some threads look different, depending on where you hold the thread.

Sample of three quilted feathers

Work this stitch from left to right; come up through the quilt top (1); go down, making a stitch in the direction that you wish to go (2); and then emerge midpoint of the previous stitch (3); always keeping the working thread on the same side of the stitching line.

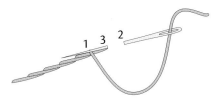

Chain Stitch or Lazy Daisy

I've always liked this stitch so much that I signed many of my early quilts using this stitch with doubled quilting thread.

For this stitch, come up through the quilt top (1) and form a loop. Go back down (2) next to the spot where the thread emerged; then come back up (3), making a stitch the desired length, make a loop, and go down again (4). Repeat to make a chain. Lazy daisies are just chain stitches that aren't connected.

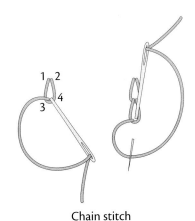

Chain stitch

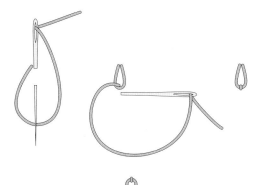

Lazy daisy stitch

French Knot

If you don't have any beads, or prefer not to use beads, you can use French knots instead.

Bring the needle up through quilt top (1). Wrap the thread twice around the needle (for a larger knot wrap the thread more times or use thicker thread). Insert the needle back down close to, but not in the same place (2). Holding the knot, pull the thread tight.

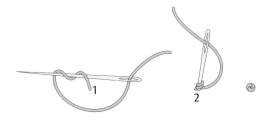

Hand Beading

I like to work from the quilt front after the quilting has been completed. If you plan to place beads near the binding, I highly recommend that the binding is attached before beading. I've found nylon beading thread to work the best for me, and I prefer either C-Lon or Silamide, although I've also used Nymo.

Protect the Thread

Bugle beads (or other similar beads) have rough edges that can cut the thread over time. To protect the thread, place a seed bead on each end of the bugle bead when sewing it in place.

1. Thread your needle with nylon beading thread, double the thread, and knot both ends together. Insert the needle in the top layer near where you want to place the bead, and sew through the top two layers only (the quilt top and batting). Pull the needle out at the point where you want to place the bead and gently pull the thread until the knot pops through the fabric and into the batting. If the knot is too large, or if the fabric is too closely woven, you may need to either leave the knot showing on the back (not my preference), or you can use tiny backstitches that will be hidden under the beads, to secure the thread. Always pull on the thread to test your backstitches, making sure they're secure.

2. Pick up a bead with the needle and slide it down the thread to the fabric. Insert the needle into the fabric and batting close to the bead and make a backstitch, coming back up through the two layers in the same place you started.

3. Insert the needle through the bead again and into the top two layers, and then emerge where you want the next bead to be placed. Repeat step 2 to sew on the next bead.

4. To end your thread, tie a knot close to the fabric and insert the needle into the top two layers. Pull the needle out and gently pull the thread until the knot pops through the fabric and into the batting; cut the thread at the quilt's surface. Or you can make several very tiny backstitches, but make sure the thread is secure before cutting the thread.

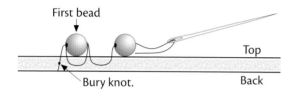

Binding

I prefer to sew the binding to the front of the quilt, and then finish by hand sewing the binding to the quilt back. Occasionally, I will bind a quilt completely by machine. Then I sew the binding to the back of the quilt and fold it to the quilt front, so I can see to cover the line of stitches on the front of the quilt. I then use a decorative stitch such as a feather or blanket stitch along the folded edge.

Cut the required number of 2¼"-wide binding strips for your project. Follow these steps to sew the binding strips together and onto the quilt:

1. Place the strips at right angles and sew across the corner as shown. Trim the excess fabric, leaving a generous ¼" seam allowance, and press the seam allowances open.

   Note: If you're using a striped fabric, the binding will look better if you use a straight seam, matching up the stripes as best you can, so you don't interrupt the pattern.

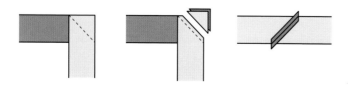

2. Press the long binding strip in half lengthwise, wrong sides together and raw edges aligned.

3. Starting along one side, align the raw edge of the binding with the edge of the quilt. Leaving an 8" to 10" tail of binding, start sewing using a ¼" seam allowance. Stop sewing ¼" from the corner; back-stitch and remove the quilt from the machine.

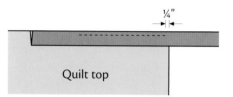

4. Turn the quilt; fold the binding straight up and away from the quilt, and then fold it down, aligning the raw edges with the edge of the quilt top. Begin sewing at the folded edge and continue down the next side of the quilt, stopping ¼" from the next corner.

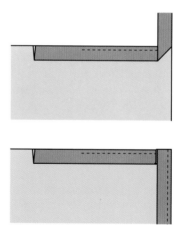

5. Repeat the mitering process at each corner. Stop stitching about 10" from the point where you started. Overlap the beginning and ending tails of the binding. Mark the binding strips so that the overlap is 2¼" (or the width of your cut binding). Trim each end of the binding at the marked points.

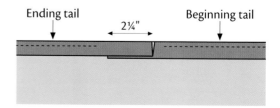

6. Unfold both ends of the binding strip, and then align them at right angles, right sides together as shown. Pin the ends together, and then sew diagonally from corner to corner. Trim the excess fabric, leaving a generous ¼" seam allowance, and press the seam allowances open. Refold the binding strip; press and sew it in place on the quilt.

7. Fold the binding to the back of the quilt. Hand stitch in place, folding the miters as you reach each corner.

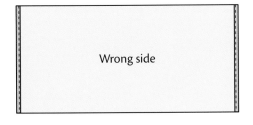

Quilt back

Hanging Sleeve

1. Measure the width of your quilt. From your leftover backing fabric (or a different fabric), cut a piece of fabric to that length and a width of 8½".

2. On the wrong side, mark lines ⅞" and 1½" from the raw edge on the both short ends of the fabric strip. On each end, fold the raw edge to the ⅞" mark; press. Fold again, aligning the folded edge with the 1½" mark; press. Stitch close to the edge to make a hem on each end.

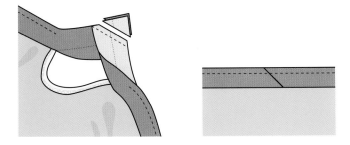

Wrong side

3. Fold the fabric in half lengthwise, *wrong* sides together. Finger crease or lightly press with a dry iron to mark the center. The creased line is only a guide.

Press fold for guide.

4. Open the fabric and fold both raw edges to meet at the pressed line, wrong sides together. Steam press both folded lines to make a permanent crease.

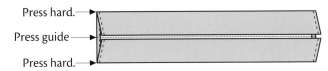

Press hard.
Press guide
Press hard.

5. Align the raw edges, wrong sides together, and sew using a ¼" seam allowance. Press the seam allowances open. The side without the seam is larger, and will be slightly bowed (or convex).

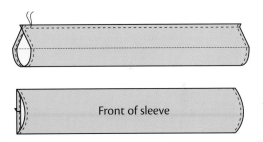

Front of sleeve

6. Place the sleeve on the back of the quilt with the seam side next to the quilt and 1" below the top edge of the binding. The sleeve will be about 1" shorter on each end than the quilt. Hand stitch the top and the bottom of the sleeve to the quilt, being careful that your stitches do not go through to the front of the quilt. Stitch the ends, making sure to keep the ends open.

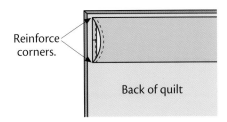

Reinforce corners.

Back of quilt

Asian Spider Mums

I wanted to make a red-and-gold quilt and decided I would use four different light fabrics for the background and a variety of deep-red Asian prints for the mums to give the quilt a calm, yet formal feel. It would also look beautiful and be very dramatic if you put bright mums on a dark indigo or black background. Or place hot flower colors, like red or yellow, on cool background fabrics, such as blue or purple, for a very exciting, vibrant look.

Materials

Yardage is based on 42"-wide fabric.

3 yards of medium cream print for sashing, outer border, and binding

7 fat quarters (or 1¾ yards *total*) of assorted red prints for flower appliqués

1 yard of cream print for blocks

¾ yard of red print for flower appliqués and inner border

⅔ yard of tan print for blocks and sashing squares

½ yard of khaki print for blocks

3⅓ yards of fabric for backing and hanging sleeve

55" x 73" piece of batting

Transparent thread (optional)

4 to 5 water-soluble glue sticks

Freezer paper

Cutting

Cut all strips across the width of the fabric unless otherwise indicated.

From the cream print, cut:
* 6 strips, 4½" x 42"; crosscut into 24 rectangles, 4½" x 8½"

From the khaki print, cut:
* 3 strips, 4½" x 42"; crosscut into 24 squares, 4½" x 4½"

From the tan print, cut:
* 2 strips, 8½" x 42"; crosscut into 6 squares, 8½" x 8½"
* 1 strip, 2½" x 42"; crosscut into 12 squares, 2½" x 2½"

From the *lengthwise grain* of the medium cream print, cut:
* 2 strips, 4½" x 74"
* 2 strips, 4½" x 56"
* 4 strips, 2¼" x 65"

From the remaining medium cream print, cut:
* 9 strips, 2½" x 42"; crosscut into 17 strips, 2½" x 16½"

From the red print for inner border, cut:
* 7 strips, 2½" x 42"

Technique Used

You'll use the following technique when making this quilt.

* Freezer-paper, glue-basted appliqué (page 13)

Assembling the Blocks

1. Sew a khaki square to each end of a cream rectangle to make unit A. Press the seam allowances toward the khaki print. Make 12 A units.

A unit.
Make 12.

2. Sew cream rectangles to opposite sides of an 8½" tan square to make unit B. Press the seam allowances toward the tan square. Make six B units.

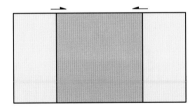

B unit.
Make 6.

3. Lay out two A units and one B unit as shown. Sew the units together and press the seam allowances toward the A units to complete the block. Make six blocks.

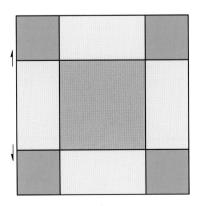

Make 6.

Pieced and quilted by Lynn Ann Majidimehr

Finished quilt: 50½" x 68½"

Finished block: 16" x 16"

Appliquéing the Blocks

Use a combination of red prints to make each flower. Three of the flowers are reversed to make the design more interesting.

1. Enlarge the pattern on page 28 and use the "Freezer-Paper, Glue-Basted Appliqué" technique to prepare three spider mums and three reversed spider mums using the red fat quarters and remaining red print.

2. Center one spider mum on each block and use a glue stick to glue baste in place; press.

3. Hand or machine appliqué the spider mums. Make six.

Assembling the Quilt Top

1. Lay out the appliquéd blocks, the 2½" x 16½" medium cream sashing strips, and the 2½" tan squares as shown in the quilt assembly diagram.

2. Sew two blocks and three vertical sashing strips together to make a block row, pressing the seam allowances toward the sashing strips. Make three block rows.

3. Sew three tan squares and two horizontal sashing strips together to make a sashing row, pressing the seam allowances toward the sashing strips. Make four sashing rows.

4. Sew the block rows and sashing rows together to complete the quilt center. Press the seam allowances toward the sashing rows.

5. Sew the 2½"-wide red strips together end to end. From the strip, cut two 74"-long strips for the side borders and two 56"-long strips for the top and bottom borders.

6. Pair a red strip with a 4½"-wide cream strip of the same length. Center and sew the strips together along their long edges. Make two side border strips, pressing the seam allowances toward the outer border. Make two border strips for the top and bottom and press the seam allowances toward the inner border.

7. Referring to "Borders with Mitered Corners" on page 15, sew the side, and then the top and bottom borders to the quilt top. Press the seam allowances toward the borders. Miter the corners, trim, and then press the seam allowances open.

Quilt assembly

Finishing the Quilt

1. Measure and cut the backing fabric into two equal lengths; then sew the lengths together using a ½" seam allowance. Trim off the selvages, leaving a ¼" seam allowance. Press the seam allowances open.

2. Layer the quilt top with batting and backing. Baste the layers together.

3. Quilt as desired, or use the quilting suggestions on page 28.

4. Using the 2¼"-wide medium cream strips and referring to "Binding" on page 22, make and attach the binding.

5. If you want to hang your quilt, add a hanging sleeve as described on page 23.

Quilting Suggestions

I took the Asian fabrics and flower style into consideration when choosing my quilting design, quilting watery swirls in the background. I stitched in the ditch around the flowers so I wouldn't flatten them. The inner border was quilted with nested teardrops to make a continuous vine.

Spider Mum
Enlarge 215%.
Make 3 and 3 reversed.
Pattern pieces do not
include seam allowances.

Watercolor Lilies

Lilies are beautiful flowers, and I wanted this quilt to look like a watercolor painting with the colors in the background pieces running from one piece into another.

Materials

Yardage is based on 42"-wide fabric.

2¼ yards of multicolored batik for sashing, outer border, and binding

1⅝ yards of light aqua batik for blocks

1¼ yards of medium green batik for blocks and inner border

⅝ yard of violet batik for sashing squares and lily appliqués

⅝ yard of pink batik for lily appliqués

⅝ yard of coral batik for lily appliqués

½ yard of teal striped batik for vase appliqué

⅛ yard of green batik for leaf appliqués

3⅓ yards of fabric for backing and hanging sleeve

55" x 73" piece of batting

Light green embroidery thread for flower centers

Light gold seed beads and gold cylinder or hex beads for flower centers

Nylon beading thread

4 to 5 water-soluble glue sticks

Freezer paper

Cutting

Cut all strips across the width of the fabric.

From the light aqua batik, cut:
* 3 strips, 16½" x 42"; crosscut into 6 squares, 16½" x 16½"

From the medium green batik, cut:
* 4 strips, 5½" x 42"; crosscut into 24 squares, 5½" x 5½"
* 6 strips, 2½" x 42"

From the multicolored batik, cut:
* 7 strips, 5½" x 42"
* 7 strips, 2¼" x 42"
* 9 strips, 2" x 42"; crosscut into 17 strips, 2" x 16½"

From the violet batik, cut:
* 1 strip, 2" x 42"; crosscut into 12 squares, 2"x 2"

Techniques Used

You'll use the following techniques when making this quilt.

* Freezer-paper, glue-basted appliqué (page 13)
* Embroidery (page 20)
* Hand beading (page 21)

Assembling the Blocks

1. Draw a diagonal line from corner to corner on the wrong side of the medium green squares. Place a marked square on one corner of a light aqua square, right sides together, and stitch along the marked line as shown. Trim away the corner fabric, leaving a ¼" seam allowance, and press the resulting triangle open.

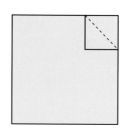 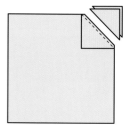

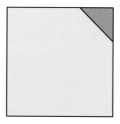

2. Repeat step 1, sewing medium green squares to the remaining three corners to complete the block. Make six blocks.

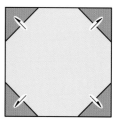

Make 6.

Pieced and quilted by Lynn Ann Majidimehr

Finished quilt: 51" x 68½"

Finished block: 16" x 16"

Appliquéing the Blocks

1. Enlarge the pattern on page 33, and use the "Freezer-Paper, Glue-Basted Appliqué" technique to prepare six lily vases. Use the green batik for the leaves; the pink, violet, and coral batiks for the lilies; and the teal striped batik for the vases.

2. Center one lily vase on each block and use a glue stick to glue baste in place; press.

3. Hand or machine appliqué the lily vases. Make six.

Assembling the Quilt Top

1. Lay out the appliquéd blocks, the multicolored 2" x 16½" strips, and the violet squares as shown in the quilt assembly diagram.

2. Sew two blocks and three vertical sashing strips together to make a block row, pressing the seam allowances toward the sashing strips. Make three block rows.

3. Sew three violet squares and two horizontal sashing strips together to make a sashing row, pressing the seam allowances toward the sashing strips. Make four sashing rows.

4. Sew the block rows and sashing rows together to complete the quilt center. Press the seam allowances toward the sashing rows.

5. Sew the 2½"-wide medium green strips together end to end. From the strip, cut two 74"-long side-border strips and two 56"-long strips for the top and bottom borders.

6. Sew the 5½"-wide multicolored strips together end to end. From the strip, cut two 74"-long side-border strips and two 56"-long strips for the top and bottom borders.

7. Pair a green inner-border strip with a multicolored outer-border strip of the same length. Center and sew the strips together along their long edges. Make two side border strips, pressing the seam allowances toward the outer border. Make two border strips for the top and bottom borders and press the seam allowances toward the inner border.

8. Referring to "Borders with Mitered Corners" on page 15, sew the side, and then the top and bottom borders to the quilt top. Press the seam allowances toward the borders. Miter the corners, trim, and then press the seam allowances open.

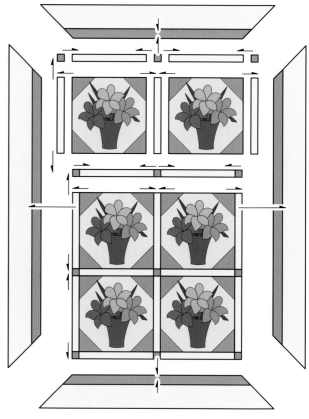

Quilt assembly

Finishing the Quilt

1. Measure and cut the backing fabric into two equal lengths; then sew the lengths together using a ½" seam allowance. Trim off the selvages, leaving a ¼" seam allowance. Press the seam allowances open.

2. Layer the quilt top with batting and backing. Baste the layers together.

3. Quilt as desired, or use the quilting suggestions on page 33.

4. Using the 2¼"-wide multicolored binding strips and referring to "Binding" on page 22, make and attach the binding.

5. If you want to hang your quilt, add a hanging sleeve as described on page 23.

Quilting and Embroidery Suggestions

To keep the focus on the flowers, the block background was quilted with a simple stipple. Leafy vines were quilted in the corner triangles, and the flowers were stitched with lines coming from the center to give them some dimension. The sashing strips and squares were quilted with swirls. The inner border was quilted with nested teardrops to give the illusion of a vine; lastly, the outer border was quilted with a combination of anything and everything, so that anyone who looks at the quilt closely will have something to explore.

Once the quilting was finished, outline stitches were embroidered in the center of each lily with beads at the ends to make the flower appear more lifelike.

Embroidery and bead placement

Lily Vase
Enlarge 200%.
Make 6.
Pattern pieces do not
include seam allowances.

Jeweled Orchids

When I was young, my mother loved to grow orchids. There were all different types, and the cattleyas were always my favorites, so I thought it would be nice to make a quilt to remember them.

Materials

Yardage is based on 42"-wide fabric.

2⅛ yards of purple batik for Orchid block background, outer border, and binding

1 yard of green striped batik for inner border and leaf appliqués

⅔ yard of dark green batik for Diamond in a Square blocks and stem and leaf appliqués

⅔ yard of dark pink batik for Nine Patch blocks, orchid appliqués, and middle border

½ yard of medium green batik for Nine Patch blocks

½ yard of light peach batik for orchid appliqués

⅜ yard of lime green batik for Diamond in a Square blocks

¼ yards of orange spotted batik for orchid appliqués

¼ yard of yellow batik for orchid appliqués

⅛ yard of light yellow batik for orchid appliqués

⅛ yard of off-white fabric for orchid appliqués

3 yards of fabric for backing and hanging sleeve

49" x 55" piece of batting

¾ yard of 20"-wide lightweight fusible web

Freezer paper

Parchment paper

2 to 3 water-soluble glue sticks

Cutting

Cut all strips across the width of the fabric.

From the medium green batik, cut:
* 10 strips, 1½" x 42"

From the dark pink batik, cut:
* 8 strips, 1½" x 42"
* 6 strips, ¾" x 42"

From the lime green batik, cut:
* 4 strips, 2⅝" x 42"; crosscut into 50 squares, 2⅝" x 2⅝"

From the dark green batik, cut:
* 7 strips, 2⅜" x 42"; crosscut into 100 squares, 2⅜" x 2⅜". Cut squares in half diagonally to yield 200 triangles.

From the green striped batik, cut:
* 6 strips, 1½" x 42"

From the purple batik, cut:
* 6 strips, 3½" x 42"
* 6 strips, 2¼"x 42"
* 1 square, 20" x 20"
* 2 squares, 14" x 14"

Techniques Used

You'll use the following techniques when making this quilt.

* Freezer-paper, glue-basted appliqué (page 13)

* Fusible appliqué (page 12)

Assembling the Nine Patch Blocks

1. Sew a medium green strip to each long side of a dark pink strip to make strip set A; press the seam allowances toward the medium green strip. Make four strip sets. Crosscut the strip sets into 100 segments, 1½" wide.

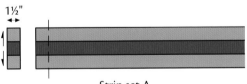

Strip set A.
Make 4. Cut 100 segments.

2. Sew a dark pink strip to each long side of a medium green strip to make strip set B; press the seam allowances toward the medium green strip. Make two strip sets. Crosscut the strip sets into 50 segments, 1½" wide.

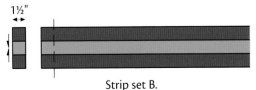

Strip set B.
Make 2. Cut 50 segments.

Pieced and quilted by Lynn Ann Majidimehr

Finished quilt: 45" x 51"

Finished Nine Patch block: 3" x 3"

Finished Diamond in a Square block: 3" x 3"

Finished Orchid blocks: 12" x 12" and 18" x 18"

3. Arrange two A segments and one B segment as shown. Sew the segments together to make a Nine Patch block; press. Make 50 blocks.

Make 50.

Assembling the Diamond in a Square Blocks

1. Sew dark green triangles to opposite sides of a lime green square. Press the seam allowances toward the triangles.

2. Sew a dark green triangle to each of the two remaining sides of the lime green square to complete a Diamond in a Square block. Make 50 blocks.

Make 50.

Assembling the Appliqué Blocks

I used a combination of appliqué techniques to make the Orchid blocks; however, you may wish to fuse all the pieces to the background. I assembled the larger pieces using the "Freezer-Paper, Glue-Basted Appliqué" technique. In the center area I used the "Fusible Appliqué" technique, because it would have been nearly impossible to turn the edges on the tiny pieces.

1. Enlarge the pattern on page 40 and trace pieces 1–11 and the B background pieces as one unit onto the dull side of freezer paper. Make one 18" Orchid block. Cut out the pieces on the traced lines and set aside the background pieces. Using the "Freezer-Paper, Glue-Basted Appliqué" technique and the green striped, dark green, light peach, and orange spotted batiks, prepare the pieces. Refer to the photo as needed for color placement guidance. Glue the flower pieces together to create an outer-flower unit.

2. Arrange the outer-flower unit on the 20" purple batik square using the freezer-paper background pieces to make sure there is about 1" of purple batik beyond the pieces all around the block. (The freezer-paper background pieces will help center the flower so that the block can be squared up and trimmed to size later.) Glue baste the outer-flower unit and leaves to the background. Remove the freezer paper.

3. Carefully cut away the purple from underneath the flower unit, leaving a scant ¼" seam allowance.

4. The inner flower is constructed using the "Fusible Appliqué" technique. Trace pieces 12–18 onto the dull side of freezer paper, making sure to leave about ½" of space between the pieces. Again referring to the photo for color placement guidance and using the off-white, light yellow, yellow, and dark pink batiks, apply fusible web to the wrong side of the fabrics, and then cut out the pieces. To make the inner-flower unit, place parchment paper on top of the placement guide, and then assemble the pieces on top of the parchment paper.

5. Working on a pressing surface covered with parchment paper, place the inner-flower unit on top of the outer-flower unit, making sure the seam allowances overlap the outer-flower unit. Fuse in place.

6. Remove the block from the parchment paper. Sew around the fused and turned edges using matching thread and a narrow zigzag stitch. You may wish to pin parchment paper to the back of the block to keep from accidentally fusing it when constructing the quilt top. (Be sure to remove the paper before basting the quilt layers together. The flower center may be fused to the batting before quilting if desired.) Make one block. Square up the block to measure 18½" x 18½", centering the design in the middle of the square.

7. Repeat steps 1–6 to make two 12" Orchid blocks using the 14" purple batik squares. Square up the blocks to measure 12½" x 12½".

Assembling the Quilt Top

The quilt is made from different-sized blocks, so you'll need to sew the blocks together in sections, and then join the sections together.

1. Lay out the Nine Patch blocks, Square in a Diamond blocks, and the Orchid blocks in sections as shown in the quilt assembly diagram.

2. Alternating the blocks, sew two Nine Patch blocks and two Diamond in a Square blocks together to make a four-block row. Press the seam allowances toward the Nine Patch blocks. Make four rows.

3. Referring to the diagram and photo, sew four-block rows to opposite sides of a small Orchid block, pressing the seam allowances toward the Orchid blocks. Make two of these units.

4. Alternating the blocks, sew three Nine Patch blocks and three Diamond in a Square blocks together to make a six-block row. Press the seam allowances toward the Nine Patch blocks. Make eight rows.

5. Sew a six-block row to the top of one orchid unit from step 3. Sew a six-block row to the bottom of the remaining orchid unit, pressing the seam allowances toward the Orchid blocks. Sew these two units together to make a two-orchid unit and press.

6. Again referring to the diagram, sew three of the six-block rows from step 4 together along their long edges to make a three-row unit; press. Sew the remaining six-block rows together in the same manner to make a second three-row unit.

7. Sew three-row units to opposite sides of the large Orchid block to complete the section; press.

8. Alternating the blocks, sew six Nine Patch blocks and six Diamond in a Square blocks together to make a block row; press. Make a total of three block rows. Sew a block row to the top and bottom of the large orchid unit, referring to the photo as needed.

9. Sew the remaining block row to the top of the two-orchid unit; press. Then sew the unit to the section from step 8 to complete the quilt center; press.

Quilt assembly

Adding the Borders

1. Sew the green striped batik strips together end to end. From the strip, cut two 56"-long strips for the side borders and two 50"-long strips for the top and bottom borders.

2. Repeat step 1 using the ¾"-wide dark pink strips for the middle border, and then the 3½"-wide purple strips for outer border.

3. Using an inner-border strip, a middle-border strip, and an outer-border strip of the same length, center and sew the strips together along their long edges. Make two side border strips, pressing the seam allowances toward the outer border. Make two border strips for the top and bottom borders and press the seam allowances toward the inner border.

4. Referring to "Borders with Mitered Corners" on page 15, sew the side, and then the top and bottom borders to the quilt top. Press the seam allowances toward the borders. Miter the corners, trim, and then press the seam allowances open.

Finishing the Quilt

1. Measure and cut the backing fabric into two equal lengths; then sew the lengths together using a ½" seam allowance. Trim off the selvages, leaving a ¼" seam allowance. Press the seam allowances open.

2. Layer the quilt top with batting and backing. Baste the layers together.

3. Quilt as desired, or use the quilting suggestions below.

4. Using the 2¼"-wide purple strips and referring to "Binding" on page 22, make and attach the binding.

5. If you want to hang your quilt, add a hanging sleeve as described on page 23.

Quilting Suggestions

To keep the focus on the flowers, the block background was quilted with a simple stipple. The flowers were heavily stitched with contour lines to give them dimension similar to real orchids. The blocks were quilted with a variety of swirls, tiny feathers, leafy branches, and other designs created to fit the blocks. The outer border was quilted with simple nested teardrops so it won't distract from the quilt center.

Orchid
Enlarge 200% for 12" block.
Make 2.
Enlarge 300% for 18" block.
Make 1.
Pattern pieces do not
include seam allowances.

Summer Floral Table Runner

Real flowers don't last very long, usually only a week at best, and I wanted flowers that last longer. By stitching flowers on a table runner, I can have flowers that last much longer than the real thing! I had so much fun making this one, that I made two more using different color combinations. All three table runners can be found on page 9.

Materials

Yardage is based on 42"-wide fabric.

1⅜ yards of aqua batik for Four Patch blocks, outer border, and binding

¾ yard of dark green batik for stem and swirl appliqués

¾ yard *total* of assorted yellow fabrics for sunflower petal and daisy center appliqués

½ yard of pink batik for Four Patch blocks

⅜ yard of bright green batik for sunflower leaf appliqués

⅓ yard of pink striped batik for inner border

⅓ yard of dark pink batik for daisy appliqués

¼ yard of medium green batik for ivy leaf appliqués

3 squares, 6" x 6", of dark yellow batik for sunflower center appliqués

1¾ yards of fabric for backing

29" x 59" piece of batting

4 yards of 20"-wide fusible web

Freezer paper

Parchment paper

Cutting

Cut all strips across the width of the fabric.

From the aqua batik, cut:
* 5 strips, 3½" x 42"
* 5 strips, 3" x 42"
* 5 strips, 2¼" x 42"

From the pink batik, cut:
* 5 strips, 3" x 42"

From the pink striped batik, cut:
* 5 strips, 1½" x 42"

From the dark green batik cut:
* 1 square, 12" x 15"

Technique Used

You'll use the following technique when making this quilt.

* Fusible appliqué (page 12)

Assembling the Blocks

1. Sew a 3"-wide aqua strip and pink strip together along their long edges to make a strip set. Make a total of five strip sets. Press the seam allowances toward the pink strip. Cut the strip sets into 54 segments, 3" wide.

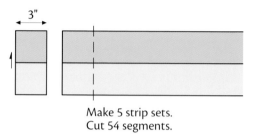

Make 5 strip sets.
Cut 54 segments.

2. Sew two segments together to make a Four Patch block. Make 27 blocks.

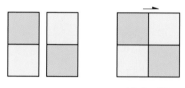

Make 27.

Assembling the Quilt Top

1. Lay out the blocks in nine rows of three blocks each. Sew the blocks together into rows, pressing the seam allowances in opposite directions from one row to the next. Sew the rows together and press the seam allowances in one direction.

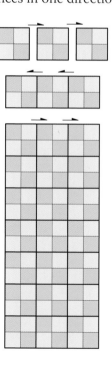

Pieced and quilted by Lynn Ann Majidimehr

Finished quilt: 23½" x 53½"

Finished block: 5" x 5"

2. Sew three of the pink striped 1½"-wide strips together end to end. Cut this strip in half to make two pieces of equal length for the side inner borders. Set aside the two remaining strips for the top and bottom borders.

3. Sew three of the 3½"-wide aqua strips together end to end. Cut this strip in half to make two pieces of equal length for the side outer borders. Set aside the two remaining strips for the top and bottom borders.

4. Pair an inner-border strip with an outer-border strip of the same length. Center and sew the strips together along their long edges. Make two side border strips, pressing the seam allowances toward the outer border. Make two border strips for the top and bottom borders and press the seam allowances toward the inner border.

5. Referring to "Borders with Mitered Corners" on page 15, sew the side, and then the top and bottom borders to the quilt top. Press the seam allowances toward the borders. Miter the corners, trim, and then press the seam allowances open.

Adding the Appliqué

1. Apply fusible web to the wrong side of the 12" x 15" dark green rectangle and cut two ⅜" x 15" bias strips for stems. Set aside the remaining fused dark green batik to use for other appliqués.

2. Using the patterns on pages 45–47 and the "Fusible Appliqué" technique, prepare 13 dark pink daisies, 13 yellow daisy centers, three bright green sunflower leaves, one reversed bright green sunflower leaf, eight medium green ivy leaves, and seven dark green swirls. Make one of each sunflower center using the dark yellow batik squares. Use the assorted yellow fabrics to make the number of petals indicated for each sunflower. Make one of each sunflower. The sunflower leaf vein, stems, and some of the swirls can be made from the fused dark green batik left over from step 1.

3. Referring to the photo on page 43 and the placement guide, arrange the prepared shapes on the quilt top using the Four Patch blocks to help with alignment. Position the largest pieces first, and then add the smaller pieces, tucking them underneath the other pieces as needed.

4. Once you're satisfied with the placement, fuse the appliqués in place on the quilt top.

Placement guide

Finishing the Quilt

1. Measure and cut the backing fabric into two equal lengths; then sew the lengths together using a ½" seam allowance. Trim off the selvages, leaving a ¼" seam allowance. Press the seam allowances open.

2. Layer the quilt top with batting and backing. Baste the layers together.

3. Quilt as desired, or use the quilting suggestions on page 45.

4. Using the 2¼"-wide aqua strips and referring to "Binding" on page 22, make and attach the binding.

5. If you want to hang your quilt, add a hanging sleeve as described on page 23.

Summer Floral Table Runner

Quilting Suggestions

The background and borders were quilted with a combination of leafy vines, feathers, swirl-feather flowers, nested teardrops, swirls, zigzag stippling, and basic stippling to fill in between larger shapes. Some areas were filled in with echo-quilted waves that blend in with the striped batik pattern.

The appliqués were quilted with straight stitching just inside the smooth edges and a free-motion zigzag around the leaves, changing the angle to fit with the leaf shape.

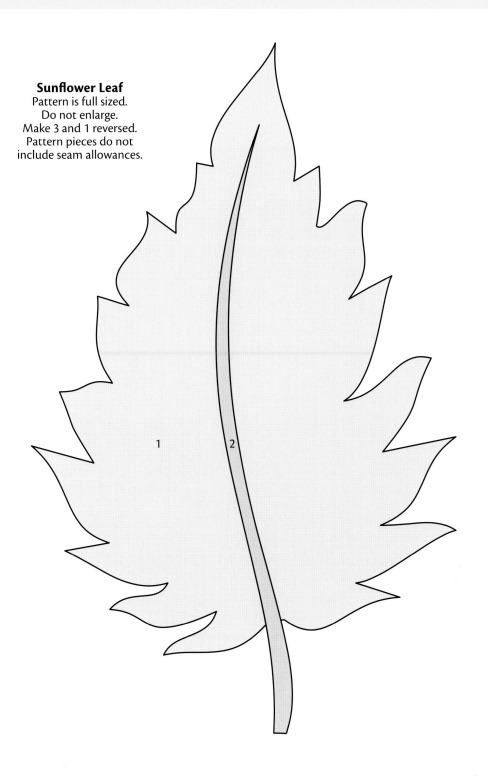

Sunflower Leaf
Pattern is full sized.
Do not enlarge.
Make 3 and 1 reversed.
Pattern pieces do not
include seam allowances.

1

2

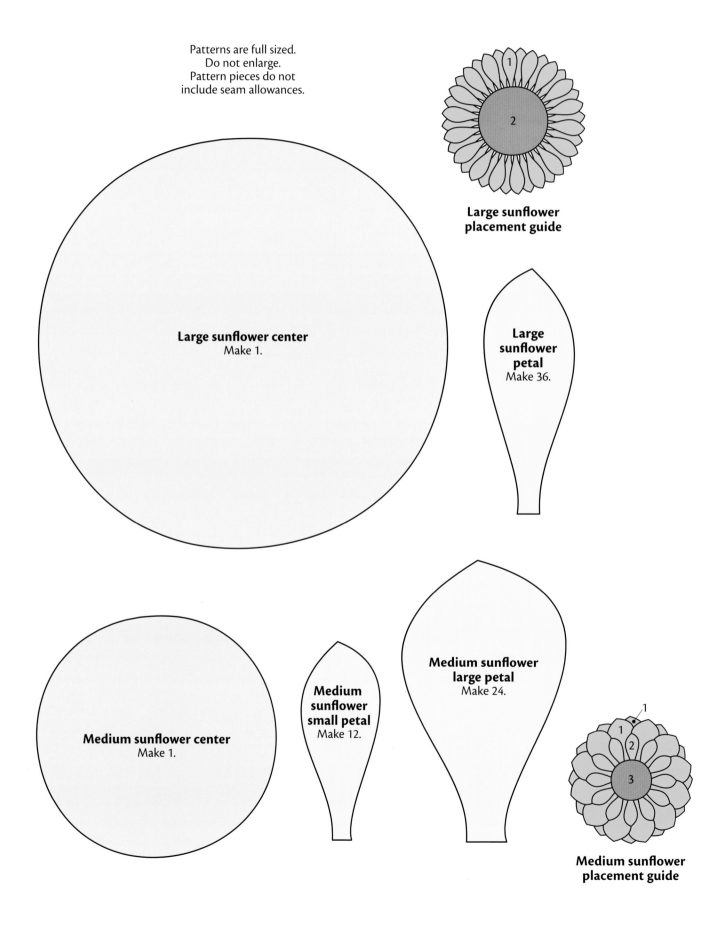

Patterns are full sized.
Do not enlarge.
Pattern pieces do not
include seam allowances.

**Large sunflower
placement guide**

Large sunflower center
Make 1.

**Large
sunflower
petal**
Make 36.

**Medium sunflower
large petal**
Make 24.

Medium sunflower center
Make 1.

**Medium
sunflower
small petal**
Make 12.

**Medium sunflower
placement guide**

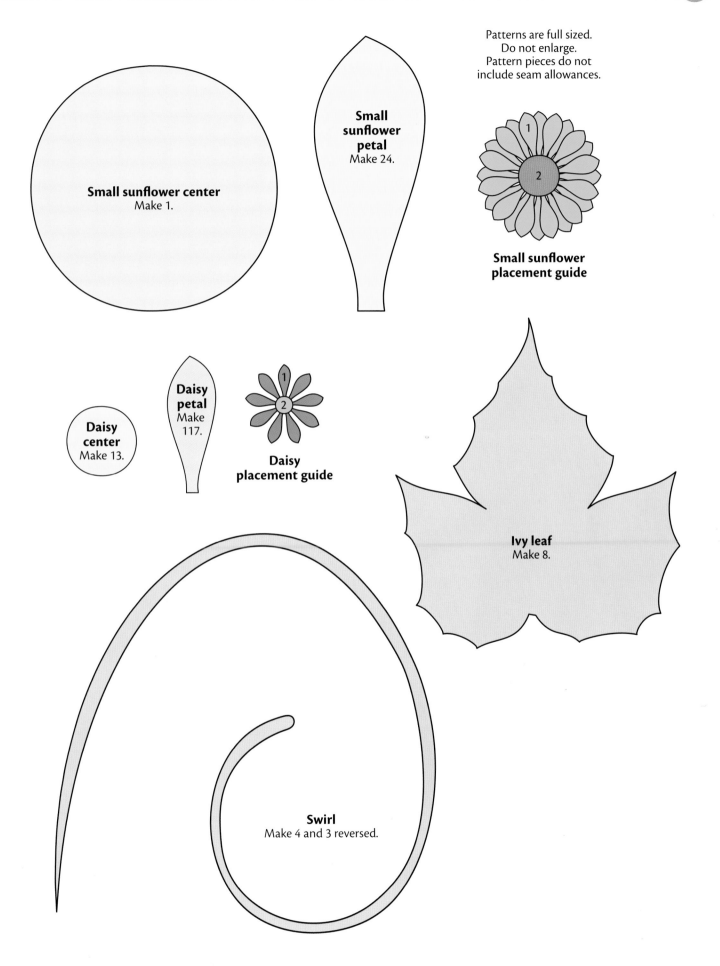

Small sunflower center
Make 1.

Small sunflower petal
Make 24.

Patterns are full sized.
Do not enlarge.
Pattern pieces do not
include seam allowances.

Small sunflower placement guide

Daisy center
Make 13.

Daisy petal
Make 117.

Daisy placement guide

Ivy leaf
Make 8.

Swirl
Make 4 and 3 reversed.

Plaid Clematis

When I think of the clematis flowers we had in a previous garden, I remember them growing on a wood-and-wire fence, not something that would make a wonderful picture, or quilt. However, when playing with quilt blocks on the computer, I tried using a plaid design for the background, which gave me the feeling of a garden fence and looked much better.

Materials

Yardage is based on 42"-wide fabric.

1⅛ yards of black batik for block, outer border, and binding

⅝ yard of cream print for block background

⅜ yard of green 1 fabric for nine-patch units and inner border

⅜ yard of magenta batik for accent border and flower appliqués

¼ yard of pink blush batik for flower appliqués

¼ yard of green 2 fabric for leaf appliqués

⅛ yard of green 3 fabric for stem appliqués

⅛ yard of light green for leaf vein and flower center appliqués

⅛ yard of pale yellow for flower center appliqués

1⅜ yards of fabric for backing and hanging sleeve

36" x 36" piece of batting

1½ yards of 20"-wide fusible web

Freezer paper

Parchment paper

Cutting

Cut all strips across the width of the fabric.

From the cream print, cut:
* 1 strip, 3½" x 42"; crosscut into 4 rectangles, 3½" x 10"
* 2 strips, 1¼" x 42"
* 1 square, 10" x 10"
* 4 squares, 3½" x 3½"

From the black batik, cut:
* 4 strips, 4½" x 42"
* 4 strips, 2¼" x 42"
* 4 strips, 1¼" x 42"
* 4 strips, 1¼" x 21" (1 will be extra)

From the green 1 fabric, cut:
* 4 strips, 2" x 42"
* 4 strips, 1¼" x 21" (1 will be extra)

From the magenta batik, cut:
* 4 strips, ¾" x 42"

From the green 3 fabric, cut:
* 1 rectangle, 1" x 18"

Technique Used

You'll use the following technique when making this quilt.

* Fusible appliqué (page 12)

Assembling the Quilt Center

The quilt center goes together quickly because it's just one big block and is assembled using strip-piecing methods.

1. Sew a 1¼" x 42" black strip to each long side of a 1¼" x 42" cream strip to make a strip set. Press the seam allowances toward the black strips. Make two strip sets. From the strip sets, cut four 10"-wide segments and label them unit A. Then cut eight 3½"-wide segments; label these unit B.

Make 2 strip sets.
Cut 4 segments, 10" wide,
and 8 segments, 3½" wide.

2. Sew a 1¼" x 21" black strip to each long side of a 1¼" x 21" green 1 strip to make a strip set. Press the seam allowances toward the black strips. From the strip set, cut four 1¼"-wide segments.

Make 1 strip set.
Cut 4 segments.

3. Sew a 1¼" x 21" green 1 strip to each long side of a 1¼" x 21" black strip to make a strip set. Press the seam allowances toward the black strips. From this strip set, cut eight 1¼"-wide segments.

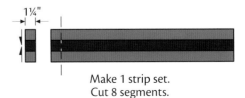

Make 1 strip set.
Cut 8 segments.

Pieced and quilted by Lynn Ann Majidimehr
Finished quilt: 32" x 32"

4. Sew a segment from step 3 to each side of a segment from step 2 as shown to make a nine-patch unit, pressing the seam allowances toward the center segment. Make four units.

Make 4.

5. Lay out four 3½" cream squares, four 3½" x 10" cream rectangles, eight B units, four A units, four nine-patch units, and the 10" cream square as shown in the quilt layout diagram.

6. Sew the pieces together in rows, pressing the seam allowances in the direction indicated by the arrows.

7. Sew the rows together and press the seam allowances toward the black strips.

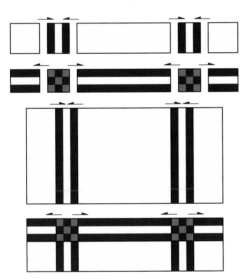

Quilt layout

Adding the Borders

1. Sew one 2"-wide green 1 strip, one ¾"-wide magenta strip, and one 4½"-wide black strip together along their long sides as shown to make a border strip. Make two side border strips, pressing the seam allowances toward the black outer border. Make two border strips for the top and bottom borders and press the seam allowances toward the green inner border.

Make 4.

2. Referring to "Borders with Mitered Corners" on page 15, sew the side, and then the top and bottom borders to the quilt top. Press the seam allowances toward the borders. Miter the corners, trim, and then press the seam allowances open.

Adding the Appliqué

1. Use the patterns on pages 52 and 53 and the "Fusible Appliqué" technique to prepare five clematis flowers and three leaves. For the flowers, use the magenta batik for the outer petals, the pink blush batik for the inner petals, the pale yellow batik for the large flower centers, and the light green batik for the small flower centers. For the leaves, use green 2 for the leaf and light green for the vein.

2. Apply fusible web to the wrong side of the 1" x 18" green 3 rectangle; cut one ⅜" x 18" rectangle and three ¼" x 8" rectangles for stems.

3. Referring to the photo on page 50 and the placement guide, arrange the flowers, leaves, and stems on the quilt top, starting with the stems from step 2. Position the largest pieces next, and then add the smaller pieces, tucking them underneath the other pieces as needed. Trim away the extra length from the stems as needed.

4. Once you're satisfied with the placement, fuse the appliqués in place on the quilt top.

Placement guide

Finishing the Quilt

1. Measure and cut the backing fabric into two equal lengths; then sew the lengths together using a ½" seam allowance. Trim off the selvages, leaving a ¼" seam allowance. Press the seam allowances open.

2. Layer the quilt top with batting and backing. Baste the layers together.

3. Quilt as desired, or use the quilting suggestions at right.

4. Using the 2¼"-wide black strips and referring to "Binding" on page 22, make and attach the binding.

5. If you want to hang your quilt, add a hanging sleeve as described on page 23.

Quilting Suggestions

The flowers and leaves were quilted with veins and the center was quilted with lines radiating from the center to make it look fluffy and to bring the flowers alive with texture. The background was quilted in a variety of swirls, swirl-centered flowers, tendrils, and tiny circles in the red batik border.

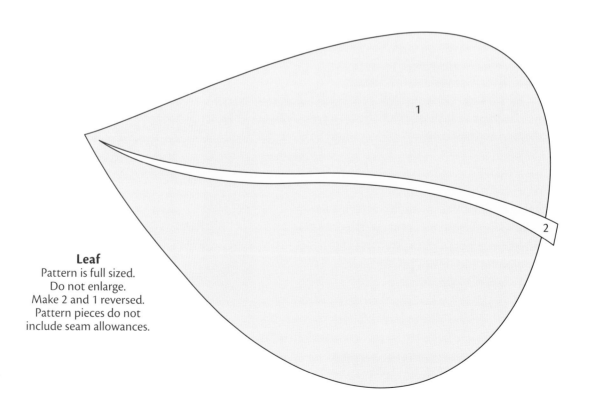

1

2

Leaf
Pattern is full sized.
Do not enlarge.
Make 2 and 1 reversed.
Pattern pieces do not
include seam allowances.

Clematis
Pattern is full sized.
Do not enlarge.
Make 5.
Pattern pieces do not
include seam allowances.

Asymmetrical Clematis

Most of my quilts are designed using a computer program, and sometimes I just play with blocks and appliqués to see what I come up with. One day I decided to play with different layouts and ended up creating this design.

Materials

Yardage is based on 42"-wide fabric.

1⅞ yards of dark green batik for outer border and binding

1⅝ yards of light green batik for blocks and appliqué background

1 yard of dark raspberry batik for middle border and flower appliqués

1 yard of dark peach mottled batik for inner border and flower appliqués

¾ yard of fuchsia multicolored batik for flower appliqués

½ yard of green geometric batik for sashing

½ yard of dark teal batik for blocks, leaf veins, and stem appliqués

½ yard of pink striped batik for blocks

⅜ yard of lime green batik for blocks and leaf appliqués

3¼ yards of fabric for backing and hanging sleeve

54" x 59" piece of batting

White YLI Pearl Crown Rayon thread for embroidered flower centers

4 yards of 20"-wide fusible web

Freezer paper

Parchment paper

Disappearing-ink marker

Cutting

Cut all strips across the width of the fabric unless otherwise indicated.

From the lime green batik, cut:
* 1 strip, 3" x 42"; crosscut into 6 rectangles, 3" x 5"

From the dark teal batik, cut:
* 1 strip, 6" x 42"
* 1 strip, 4" x 42"; crosscut into 6 rectangles, 4" x 6"
* 1 strip, 3½" x 42"; crosscut into 6 rectangles, 3½" x 5"

From the pink striped batik, cut:
* 3 strips, 4½" x 42"; crosscut into 12 rectangles, 4½" x 8"

From the light green batik, cut:
* 1 piece, 21½" x 40½"
* 1 strip, 4" x 42"; crosscut into 6 rectangles, 4" x 6"
* 1 strip, 3½" x 42"; crosscut into 6 rectangles, 3½" x 5"
* 1 strip, 3" x 42"; crosscut into 6 rectangles, 3" x 5"

From the green geometric batik, cut:
* 3 strips, 3½" x 42"; crosscut *1 of the strips* into 2 rectangles, 3½" x 8½" (set aside the remaining strips)
* 1 strip, 2½" x 42"; crosscut into 2 rectangles, 2½" x 8½"

From the dark peach mottled batik, cut:
* 6 strips, 2½" x 42"

From the dark raspberry batik, cut:
* 6 strips, ¾" x 42"

From the *lengthwise grain* of the dark green batik, cut:
* 4 strips, 5½" x 60"
* 4 strips, 2¼" x 60"

Techniques Used

You'll use the following techniques when making this quilt.

* Foundation piecing (page 9)
* Fusible appliqué (page 12)
* Embroidery (page 20)

Assembling the Blocks

1. Copy or trace the foundation pattern on page 60 onto the dull side of freezer paper. Make six copies for unit A and six reversed copies for unit B. Cut out the patterns, cutting directly on the bold outer line.

Pieced and quilted by Lynn Ann Majidimehr

Finished quilt: 50" x 55"

Finished block: 8" x 10"

2. Referring to "Foundation Piecing" instructions, make six of unit A, starting with the 3½" x 5" dark teal rectangle and the 4" x 6" light green rectangle. Then add the pink striped rectangle and lastly the 3" x 5" light green rectangle.

Unit A.
Make 6.

3. Make six of unit B starting with the 3½" x 5" light green rectangle and the 4" x 6" dark teal rectangle. Then add the pink striped rectangle and lastly the lime green rectangle.

Unit B.
Make 6.

4. Lay out two A units and two B units as shown. Sew the units together in rows, and then sew the rows together to complete the block. Make three blocks.

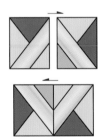

Make 3.

Assembling the Quilt Center

1. To make the vertical block row, sew a 2½" x 8½" green geometric rectangle to the short side of a block. Press the seam allowances toward the green rectangle. Make two.

2. Sew a 3½" x 8½" green geometric rectangle to each short side of the remaining block. Press the seam allowances toward the green rectangles.

3. Sew a unit from step 1 to each short side of the unit from step 2, pressing the seam allowances toward the green rectangles. The row should measure 40½" long.

4. Sew the 3½"-wide green geometric strips (including the remaining short strip) together end to end. From the strip, cut two 40½"-long strips. Sew a strip to each side of the vertical row.

5. Sew the 21½" x 40½" light green piece to the unit from step 4 to complete the quilt center.

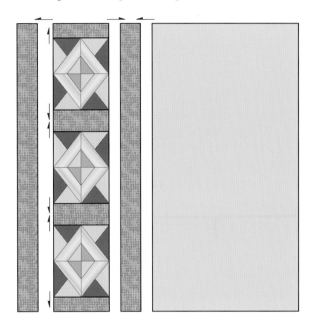

Adding the Borders

1. Sew the dark peach strips together end to end, and then cut the long strip into four equal lengths. Sew the dark raspberry strips together end to end, and then cut the long strip into four equal lengths.

2. Sew one dark peach strip, one dark raspberry strip, and one 5½"-wide dark green strip together along their long sides as shown to make a border strip. Make two side border strips, pressing the seam allowances toward the dark green outer border. Make two border strips for the top and bottom borders and press the seam allowances toward the dark peach inner border.

Make 4.

3. Referring to "Borders with Mitered Corners" on page 15, sew the side, and then the top and bottom borders to the quilt top. Press the seam allowances toward the borders. Miter the corners, trim, and then press the seam allowances open.

Adding the Appliqué

1. Enlarging the pattern on page 59 and using the "Fusible Appliqué" technique, prepare three small flowers and two large flowers. Use the fuchsia multicolored batik for the outer petals and large flower centers, the dark raspberry batik for the inner petals, and the dark peach batik for the small flower centers.

2. Use the pattern on page 61 and the lime green batik to make three leaves.

3. Apply fusible web to the wrong side of the 6"-wide dark teal strip and cut one 40"-long rectangle that is 1" wide on one end, tapering down to ½" wide on the other end. Using the remaining fused fabric, cut three 15" rectangles, tapering from ½" to ¼" wide for stems and three leaf veins using the pattern on page 61.

4. Referring to the photo on page 56 and the placement guide, arrange the flowers, leaves, and stems on the quilt top, starting with the stems from step 3. Position the largest pieces next, and then add the smaller pieces, tucking them underneath the other pieces as needed. Trim away the extra length from the stems as needed.

5. Once you're satisfied with the placement, fuse the appliqués in place on the quilt top.

Finishing the Quilt

1. Measure and cut the backing fabric into two equal lengths; then sew the lengths together using a ½" seam allowance. Trim off the selvages, leaving a ¼" seam allowance. Press the seam allowances open.

2. Layer the quilt top with batting and backing. Baste the layers together.

3. Quilt as desired, or use the quilting suggestions on page 59.

4. Use a disappearing-ink marker and the circles on page 60 to mark a small circle around the center of the small flowers and a large circle around the center of the large flowers. Using a stem or outline stitch, embroider lines radiating out from the center to the marked line.

5. Using the 2¼"-wide dark green strips and referring to "Binding" on page 22, make and attach the binding.

6. If you want to hang your quilt, add a hanging sleeve as described on page 23.

Placement guide

Quilting Suggestions

The flowers were quilted in mostly a contour style of quilting, while the leaves were quilted to add veins spreading out from the central vein. Since there was a large open area behind the clematis flowers, some feathers were quilted to give the illusion of ferns and the remainder of that area was stippled. The block sashing was quilted with swirls and the peach border quilted with a half feather. The narrow raspberry border was quilted with tiny beads and the outer border is a combination of anything I thought of at the time, fit together with a little stippling.

Clematis
Enlarge 168% for small flower.
Make 3.
Enlarge 200% for large flower.
Make 2.
Pattern pieces do not
include seam allowances.

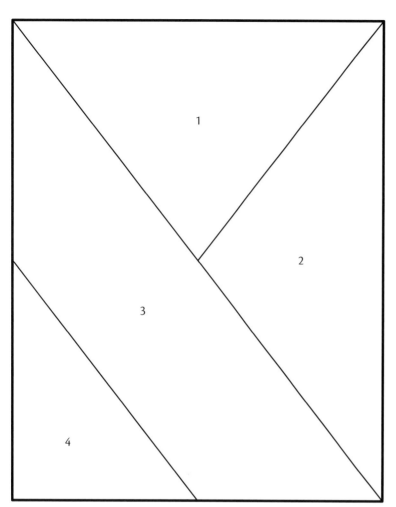

Foundation pattern
Make 6 and 6 reversed.

Patterns are full sized.
Do not enlarge.

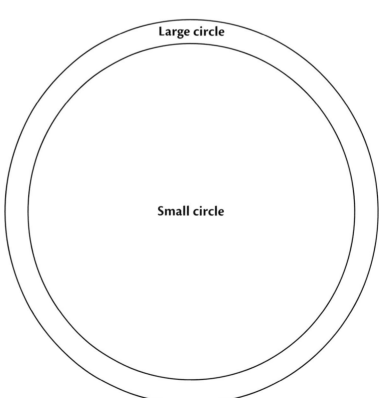

Large circle

Small circle

Leaf
Pattern is full sized.
Do not enlarge.
Make 2 and 1 reversed.
Pattern pieces do not
include seam allowances.

1

2

Summer Blooms

The first flowers that most people try to grow from seed are sunflowers, because they're easy to grow and come in quite a variety of colors and sizes. The stems of the plants aren't as beautiful as the blooms, so I've always planted them behind lower-growing flowers to hide their stems. Here I've planted my fabric sunflowers behind some cheery periwinkle, to remind me of the flowers that grew outside our front door at a previous home.

Materials

Yardage is based on 42"-wide fabric.

1⅛ yards *total* of assorted yellow fabrics for sunflower appliqués

½ yard *total* of assorted purple and pink fabrics for periwinkle appliqués

½ yard *total* of assorted green fabrics for leaf appliqués

¼ yard of golden brown batik for sunflower center appliqués

⅛ yard of pale lavender fabric for periwinkle center appliqués

⅛ yard of lavender fabric for periwinkle center appliqués

⅛ yard of dark green batik for sunflower stem and leaf vein appliqués

⅛ yard of black batik for sunflower center appliqués

¼ yard *each* of 5 blue fabrics (ranging in value from light to medium) for bargello background

¼ yard of light green fabric for bargello background

¼ yard of medium green 1 fabric for bargello background

¼ yard of medium green 2 fabric for bargello background

⅛ yard of dark green fabric for bargello background

⅞ yard of dark blue batik for inner border, outer border, and binding

¼ yard of lime green solid fabric for middle border

1½ yards of fabric for backing and hanging sleeve

37" x 37" piece of batting

3½ yards of 20"-wide fusible web

Freezer paper

Parchment paper

Cutting

Cut all strips across the width of the fabric.

From 1 of the medium blue fabrics, cut:
* 1 strip, 3½" x 42"
* 1 strip, 2" x 42"

From *each* of the 4 light to medium blue fabrics, cut:
* 2 strips, 3½" x 42" (10 total)

From the light green fabric, cut:
* 2 strips, 3½" x 42"

From the medium green 1 fabric, cut:
* 2 strips, 3½" x 42"

From the medium green 2 fabric, cut:
* 2 strips, 3½" x 42"

From the dark green fabric, cut:
* 1 strip, 2" x 42"

From the lime green solid fabric, cut:
* 4 strips, 1½" x 42"

From the dark blue batik, cut:
* 4 strips, 3½" x 42"
* 4 strips, 2¼" x 42"
* 4 strips, ¾" x 42"

From the dark green batik, cut:
* 1 strip, 2" x 42"

Technique Used

You'll use the following technique when making this quilt.

* Fusible appliqué (page 12)

Pieced and quilted by Lynn Ann Majidimehr

Finished quilt: 33" x 33"

Making the Bargello Background

The background is made from a gradation of fabrics, starting at the top with medium blue, then light blue and light green in the center, and then medium green at the bottom.

1. Lay out the 3½"-wide medium blue strip, one each of the light to medium blue strips, one light green strip, one medium green 1 strip, and one medium green 2 strip as shown. Sew the strips together along their long sides to make a strip set. Cut the strip set into 12 segments, 1½" wide. Label the segments as unit A.

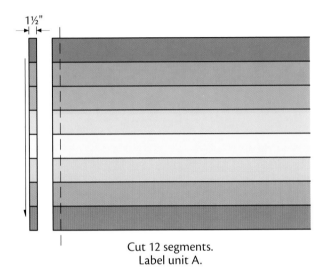

1½"

Cut 12 segments.
Label unit A.

2. Lay out the 2"-wide medium blue strip, one each of the light to medium blue strips, one light green strip, one medium green 1 strip, one medium green 2 strip, and the 2"-wide dark green strip. Sew the strips together along their long sides to make a strip set. Cut this strip set into 12 segments, 1½" wide. Label the segments as unit B.

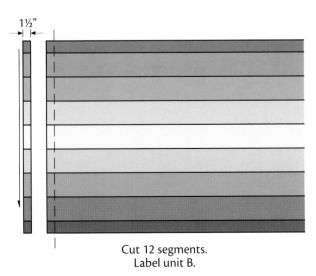

1½"

Cut 12 segments.
Label unit B.

3. Lay out the A and B units, alternating them as shown. Sew the units together to complete the bargello background. The background unit should measure 24½" x 24½".

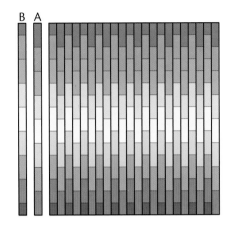

B   A

Adding the Borders

1. Sew one ¾"-wide dark blue batik strip, one 1½"-wide lime green strip, and one 3½"-wide dark blue batik strip together along their long sides to make a border strip. Make two side border strips, pressing the seam allowances toward the outer border. Make two border strips for the top and bottom borders and press the seam allowances toward the inner border.

Make 4.

2. Referring to "Borders with Mitered Corners" on page 15, sew the side, and then the top and bottom borders to the quilt top. Press the seam allowances toward the borders. Miter the corners, trim, and then press the seam allowances open.

Adding the Appliqué

1. Enlarge the pattern on page 67 and use the Fusible Appliqué technique to prepare two sunflowers and one reversed sunflower. Use the assorted yellow fabrics for the petals, the golden brown batik for the large flower center, and the black batik for the small flower center.

2. Apply fusible web to the wrong side of the dark green batik strip and cut one ⅜"-wide strip. Then cut the strip into three equal pieces for the sunflower stems.

3. Use the patterns on page 68 and the "Fusible Appliqué" technique to prepare the remaining pieces. Use the assorted green fabrics to make two sunflower leaves, two reversed sunflower leaves, 11 periwinkle leaves, and six reversed periwinkle leaves. Make 21 periwinkle flowers and six reversed periwinkle flowers using the assorted purple and pink fabrics for the petals, the pale lavender for the large flower centers, and the lavender for the small flower centers.

4. Referring to the photo on page 64 and the placement guide, arrange the sunflowers, periwinkle flowers, leaves, and stems on the quilt top, starting with the stems. Position the largest pieces next, and then add the smaller pieces, tucking them underneath the other pieces as needed. Trim away the extra length from the stems as needed.

5. Once you're satisfied with the placement, fuse the appliqués in place on the quilt top.

Placement guide

Finishing the Quilt

1. Measure and cut the backing fabric into two equal lengths; then sew the lengths together using a ½" seam allowance. Trim off the selvages, leaving a ¼" seam allowance. Press the seam allowances open.

2. Layer the quilt top with batting and backing. Baste the layers together.

3. Quilt as desired, or use the quilting suggestions below.

4. Using the 2¼"-wide dark blue batik binding strips and referring to "Binding" on page 22, make and attach the binding.

5. If you want to hang your quilt, add a hanging sleeve as described on page 23.

Quilting Suggestions

The flowers and leaves were quilted inside the appliqué edges, and quilting was used to add veins and details. The background was stippled, the narrow dark blue border was quilted with tiny circles, and nested teardrops were quilted in the lime green border. The outer border was quilted with a mix of stippling and outline quilting.

Sunflower
Enlarge 133%.
Make 2 and 1 reversed.
Pattern pieces do not
include seam allowances.

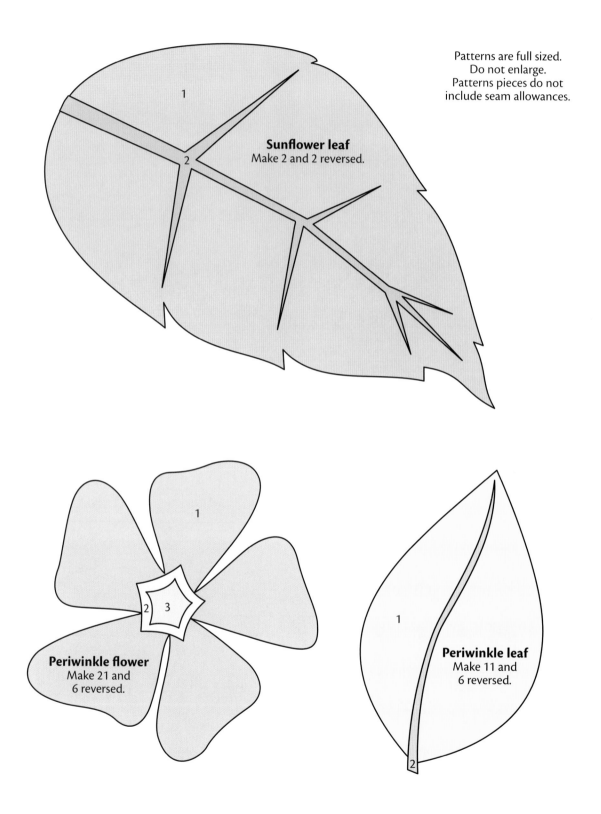

Patterns are full sized.
Do not enlarge.
Patterns pieces do not
include seam allowances.

Sunflower leaf
Make 2 and 2 reversed.

1

2

Periwinkle flower
Make 21 and
6 reversed.

1

2 3

Periwinkle leaf
Make 11 and
6 reversed.

1

2

Crepe-Paper Poppies

I remember making paper poppies in art class. I used crepe paper that stretched to make beautiful flowers on wire stems that I could give my mom for Mother's Day. The poppies in this quilt remind me of my childhood art project. Poppies come in delicate pastels, as well as bold colors that scream "look at me," and they all have beautiful details if you take a close look.

Materials

Yardage is based on 42"-wide fabric.

1½ yards of bright yellow dot batik for blocks and outer border

1¼ yards of light yellow batik for blocks and inner border

1 yard of orange batik for sashing and binding

⅛ yard of rust batik for sashing squares

1½ yards *total* of assorted raspberry and pink batiks for poppy appliqués

1 yard *total* of assorted green batiks for leaf and bud appliqués

¼ yard of green batik for stem appliqués

⅛ yard of black solid fabric for flower center appliqués

⅛ yard of lime green solid fabric for flower center appliqués

2⅞ yards of fabric for backing and hanging sleeve

46" x 60" piece of batting

4 yards of 20"-wide fusible web

Freezer paper

Parchment paper

Cutting

Cut all strips across the width of the fabric.

From the bright yellow dot batik, cut:
* 3 strips, 7¼" x 42"; crosscut into 12 squares, 7¼" x 7¼"
* 6 strips, 4½" x 42"

From the light yellow batik, cut:
* 3 strips, 7¼" x 42"; crosscut into 12 squares, 7¼" x 7¼"
* 6 strips, 2½" x 42"

From the orange batik, cut:
* 6 strips, 2¼" x 42"
* 10 strips, 1½" x 42"; crosscut into 58 strips, 1½" x 6½"

From the rust batik, cut:
* 2 strips, 1½" x 42"; crosscut into 35 squares, 1½" x 1½"

Technique Used

You'll use the following technique when making this quilt.

* Fusible appliqué (page 12)

Assembling the Blocks

1. Draw a diagonal line from corner to corner on the wrong side of each light yellow square. Layer the marked squares right sides together with the bright yellow squares and stitch ¼" on each side of the marked line. Cut the squares apart on the drawn line to make two half-square-triangle units. Press the seam allowances toward the bright yellow triangles. Make 24 units.

 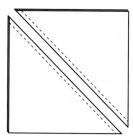

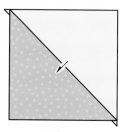

Make 24.

Pieced and quilted by Lynn Ann Majidimehr

Finished quilt: 55½" x 41½"

Finished block: 6" x 6"

2. Layer two half-square-triangle units, right sides together, so that opposite colors face each other and center seams are butted together. Mark a diagonal line on the wrong side of the top square, crossing the seam line as shown. Sew ¼" on each side of the marked line. Then cut the squares apart on the drawn line to make an Hourglass block. Press the seam allowances to one side. Make 24 blocks.

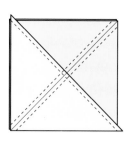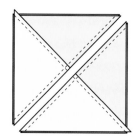

Make 24.

Assembling the Quilt Center

1. Lay out the Hourglass blocks, the orange 1½" x 6½" strips, and the rust squares as shown in the quilt assembly diagram.
2. Sew six blocks and seven vertical sashing strips together to make a block row, pressing the seam allowances toward the sashing strips. Make four block rows.
3. Sew seven rust squares and six horizontal sashing strips together to make a sashing row, pressing the seam allowances toward the sashing strips. Make five sashing rows.

4. Sew the block rows and sashing rows together to complete the quilt center. Press the seam allowances toward the sashing rows.

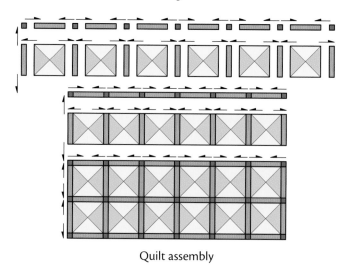

Quilt assembly

Adding the Appliqué

Some of the appliqué pieces overlap the border, while other pieces need to be stitched into the seam line, so you'll need to fuse the appliqué pieces in place before adding the borders.

1. Using the "Fusible Appliqué" technique and the patterns on pages 74–77, prepare three side poppies, two reversed side poppies, one opening poppy, two reversed opening poppies, and three full poppies using the raspberry and pink batiks for the petals, the black for the large flower centers, and the lime green for the small flower centers. Use the assorted green batiks to make one poppy bud, two reversed poppy buds, three leaves, two reversed leaves, six half leaves, and six reversed half leaves.

2. Apply fusible web to the wrong side of the green batik and cut ¼"-wide bias strips to use for stems. Piece the stems as needed by overlapping ends or tucking the ends underneath other appliqué pieces.

3. Referring to the photo on page 71, arrange the poppies, buds, leaves, and stems on the quilt top, starting with the stems. Position the largest pieces next, and then add the smaller pieces, tucking them underneath the other pieces as needed. Trim away the extra length from the stems as needed.

4. Once you're satisfied with the placement, fuse the appliqués in place, stopping about 1" from the outer edges of the quilt center. Pin any pieces that extend beyond the edge out of the way while adding the borders.

Adding the Borders

1. Sew the 2½"-wide light yellow strips together end to end. From the strip, cut two 61"-long strips for the top and bottom inner borders and two 47"-long strips for the side inner borders.

2. Sew the 4½"-wide bright yellow strips together end to end. From the strip, cut two 61"-long strips for the top and bottom borders and two 47"-long strips for the side outer borders.

3. Pair an inner-border strip with an outer-border strip of the same length. Center and sew the strips together along their long edges. Make two side border strips, pressing the seam allowances toward the outer border. Make two border strips for the top and bottom borders and press the seam allowances toward the inner border.

4. Referring to "Borders with Mitered Corners" on page 15, sew the side, and then the top and bottom borders to the quilt top. Note that some of the appliquéd pieces are sewn into the seam line. Press the seam allowances toward the borders. Miter the corners, trim, and then press the seam allowances open.

5. Fuse the overlapping appliqué pieces in place.

Placement guide

Finishing the Quilt

1. Measure and cut the backing fabric into two equal lengths; then sew the lengths together using a ½" seam allowance. Trim off the selvages, leaving a ¼" seam allowance. Press the seam allowances open.

2. Layer the quilt top with batting and backing. Baste the layers together.

3. Quilt as desired, or use the quilting suggestions below.

4. Using the 2¼"-wide orange binding strips and referring to "Binding" on page 22, make and attach the binding.

5. If you want to hang your quilt, add a hanging sleeve as described on page 23.

Quilting Suggestions

Lines giving the illusion of veins and wrinkles were quilted over the flowers and leaves, and stitching was done close to the edges to secure the raw edges of the appliquéd pieces. The background blocks were quilted with a central swirl surrounded with flames and long flame-like swirls to represent sunshine, while the sashing and cornerstones were quilted with swirls. A leafy vine with an occasional tendril fills the inner border, and ferns (pointed feathers) enter the quilt's edges; stippling fills the spaces between.

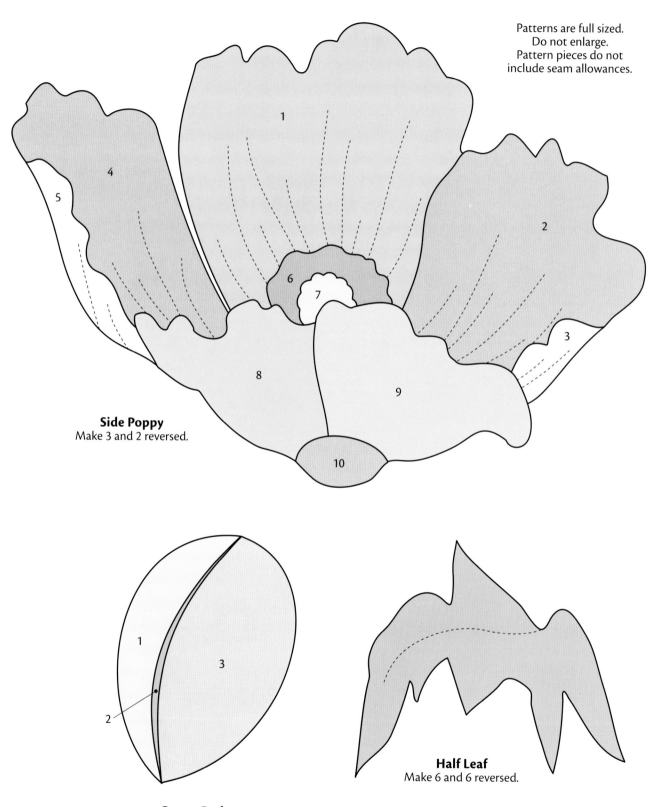

Patterns are full sized.
Do not enlarge.
Pattern pieces do not
include seam allowances.

Side Poppy
Make 3 and 2 reversed.

Poppy Bud
Make 1 and 2 reversed.

Half Leaf
Make 6 and 6 reversed.

Opening Poppy
Pattern is full sized.
Make 1 and 2 reversed.
Pattern pieces do not
include seam allowances.

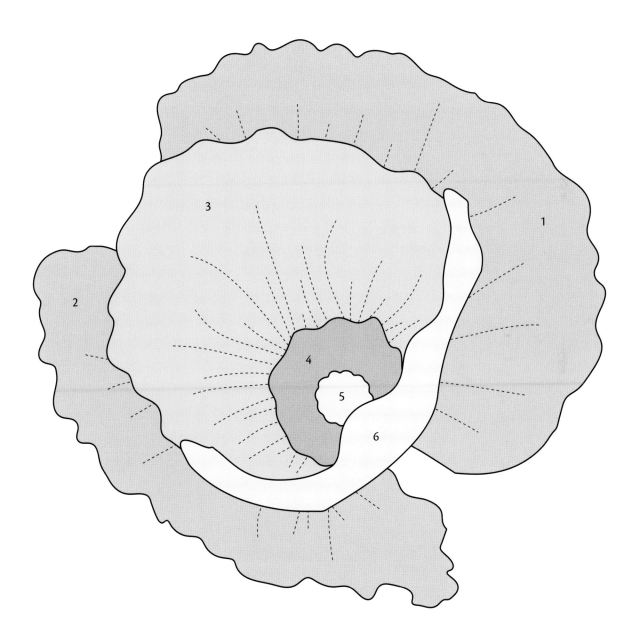

Full Poppy
Pattern is full sized.
Make 3.
Pattern pieces do not
include seam allowances.

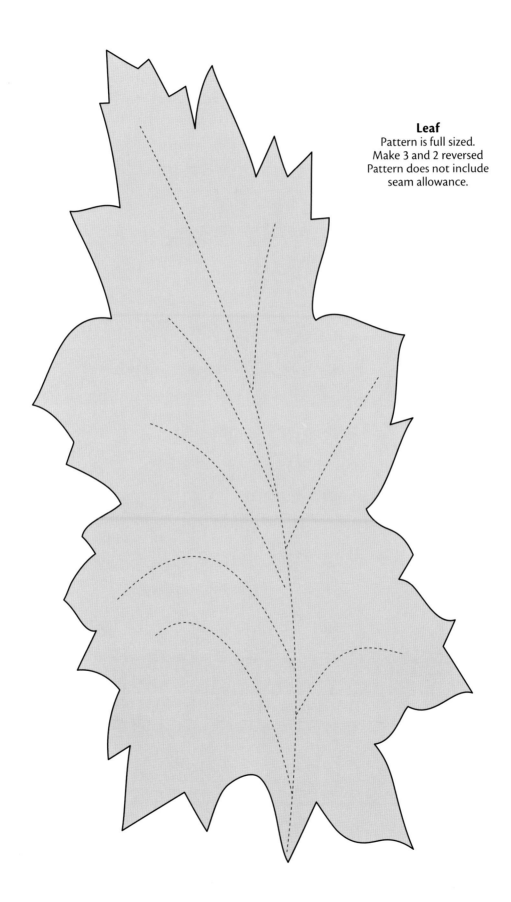

Leaf
Pattern is full sized.
Make 3 and 2 reversed
Pattern does not include
seam allowance.

Pink Dahlias

The dahlia is another of my favorite flowers! There are so many different varieties—not just colors—and the sizes vary too. You can find some that form a ball-shaped blossom, and others as large and flat as a dinner plate.

Fabric Selection

You'll need eight green fabrics, ranging in value from very light to medium or medium dark. The darkest large-scale fabric is used for the outer border, and the next-to-lightest fabric for the inner border. Arrange the green fabrics from dark to light; label the large-scale green print 1 and the other seven green prints from 2–8, with 8 being the lightest.

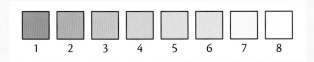

Materials

Yardage is based on 42"-wide fabric.

1⅛ yards of large-scale green fabric 1 for blocks and outer border

⅜ yard of green fabric 2 for blocks

⅜ yard of green fabric 3 for blocks

⅜ yard of green fabric 4 for blocks

¼ yard of green fabric 5 for blocks

½ yard of green fabric 6 for blocks

¾ yard of green fabric 7 for blocks and inner border

¼ yard of green fabric 8 for blocks

¾ yard of dark green batik for center medallion border, stem appliqués, and binding

¼ yard of dark pink batik for flower appliqués and middle border

½ yard *total* of assorted pink batiks for flower appliqués

¼ yard *total* of assorted bright green batiks for leaf appliqués

3 yards of fabric for backing and hanging sleeve

53" x 53" piece of batting

1½ yards of 20"-wide fusible web

Freezer paper

Parchment paper

Cutting

Cut all strips across the width of fabric.

From fabric 1, cut:
* 6 strips, 4½" x 42"
* 7 strips, 1¼" x 42"; crosscut into:
    24 rectangles, 1¼" x 5¾"
    24 rectangles, 1¼" x 5"

From fabric 2, cut:
* 8 strips, 1¼" x 42"; crosscut into:
    24 rectangles, 1¼" x 6½"
    24 rectangles, 1¼" x 5¾"

From fabric 3, cut:
* 2 strips, 1⅝" x 42"
* 6 strips, 1¼" x 42"; crosscut into:
    24 rectangles, 1¼" x 4¼"
    24 rectangles, 1¼" x 3½"

From fabric 4, cut
* 2 strips, 1⅝" x 42"
* 6 strips, 1¼" x 42"; crosscut into:
    24 rectangles, 1¼" x 5"
    24 rectangles, 1¼" x 4¼"

From fabric 5, cut:
* 2 strips, 2" x 42"; crosscut into 24 squares, 2" x 2"
* 2 strips, 1½" x 42"

From fabric 6, cut:
* 4 strips, 1⅝" x 42"
* 5 strips, 1¼" x 42"; crosscut into:
    24 rectangles, 1¼" x 3½"
    24 rectangles, 1¼" x 2¾"

From fabric 7, cut:
* 6 strips, 2" x 42"
* 4 strips, 1⅝" x 42"
* 4 strips, 1¼" x 42"; crosscut into:
    24 rectangles, 1¼" x 2¾"
    24 rectangles, 1¼" x 2"

From fabric 8, cut:
* 4 strips, 1½" x 42"

From the dark green batik, cut:
* 6 strips, 2¼" x 42"
* 1 strip, 2" x 42"
* 4 strips, 1½" x 42"

From the dark pink batik, cut:
* 6 strips, 1" x 42"

Pieced and quilted by Lynn Ann Majidimehr

Finished quilt: 48½" x 48½"

Finished block: 6" x 6"

remaining two strip sets, press the seam allowances toward fabric 7.

6		
8		
7		

Make 4.

Technique Used

You'll use the following technique when making this quilt.

✳ Fusible appliqué (page 12)

Assembling the Log Cabin Blocks

1. Sew a 1¼" x 2" fabric 7 rectangle to the 2" fabric 5 square as shown in the block diagram following step 4. Press the seam allowances toward the rectangle.

2. With the previous rectangle along the top, sew a 1¼" x 2¾" fabric 7 rectangle to the right-hand side of the unit. Press the seam allowances toward the newly added rectangle.

3. Rotate the unit 90° counterclockwise and sew a 1¼" x 2¾" fabric 6 rectangle to the right-hand side of the unit; press the seam allowances toward the newly added rectangle.

4. Continue adding rectangles to the center unit; rotating the unit 90° counterclockwise and sewing the next rectangle to the right-hand side of the unit. Press the seam allowances toward the newly added rectangle. Make 24 Log Cabin blocks.

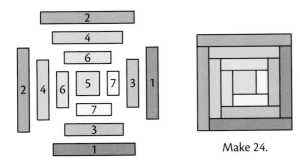

Make 24.

Assembling the Four X Blocks

1. Using 1⅝"-wide fabric 6 and 7 strips and 1½"-wide fabric 8 strips, sew one strip of *each* together along their long sides as shown to make a light green strip set. Make four strip sets. On two strip sets, press the seam allowances toward fabric 6. On the

2. Layer two strip sets right sides together, with fabrics 6 and 7 on top of each other and the seam allowances butted together. Align the 45° line on your ruler with the edge of a strip. Cut along the upper edge of the ruler to remove the corner and selvages.

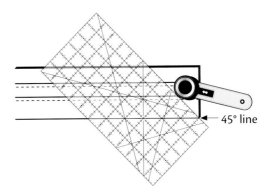

3. Rotate the ruler, place the 45° line on the ruler along the edge of a strip, and cut along the edge of the ruler to make a triangle. Continue cutting triangles from the strip set, rotating the ruler as you cut. Cut eight triangle pairs from each layered strip set (16 pairs total).

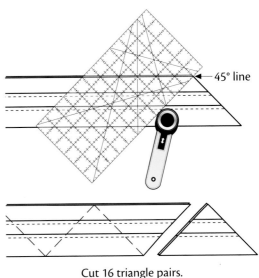

Cut 16 triangle pairs.

4. Sew each triangle pair together along one short edge, crossing the previous seams, and press the seam allowances to one side to make a half block. Make 16 light green half blocks. Trim ⅛" from both short sides of each half block, as shown.

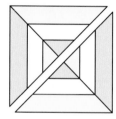
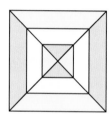

Trim.

Make 16.

5. Sew two half blocks together to make a Four X block. Make four blocks measuring 6½" x 6½". Set aside the remaining eight light green half blocks.

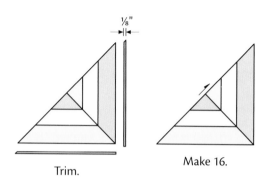

Make 4.

6. Using 1⅝"-wide fabric 3 and 4 strips and 1½"-wide fabric 5 strips, sew one strip of *each* together along their long sides as shown to make a medium green strip set. Make two strip sets. On one strip set, press the seam allowances toward fabric 3. On the remaining strip set, press the seam allowances toward fabric 4.

3
5
4

Make 2.

7. Repeat steps 2–4, cutting eight triangle pairs from the layered strip set. Then sew triangle pairs together to make eight medium green half blocks; trim.

Assembling the Quilt Center

Although this quilt top was designed with rows of blocks, it's not assembled in simple rows. I inserted a decorative flange to accent the flower-filled diamond; therefore, the quilt center is divided into sections to make the construction easier.

1. Lay out the Log Cabin blocks, Four X blocks, and the half blocks in sections as shown in the quilt assembly diagram. Make sure the blocks are oriented correctly and that the Four X blocks and light green half blocks create the center diamond.

2. To make the center diamond, sew the blocks and half blocks in rows, and then sew the rows together.

3. Fold the 1½"-wide dark green batik strips in half lengthwise, *wrong* sides together, and press. Machine baste a strip to opposite sides of the center diamond, aligning the raw edges and using a ⅛" seam allowance. Trim the excess fabric. Then baste the remaining strips to the two remaining sides.

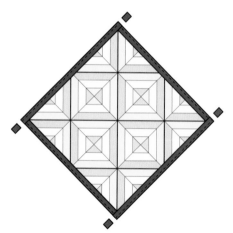

Baste and trim.

4. Sew medium green half blocks to adjacent sides of Log Cabin blocks to make triangle sections, making sure to keep the blocks oriented as shown in the diagram. Make four triangle sections and sew them to the center diamond. Press the seam allowances toward the triangle sections.

5. Sew four Log Cabin blocks together to make a block row. Make two and sew them to the sides of the section from step 4.

6. Sew six Log Cabin blocks together to make a block row. Make two and sew them to the top and bottom of the quilt center.

Quilt assembly

Adding the Appliqué

1. Use the patterns on pages 84 and 85 and the "Fusible Appliqué" technique to prepare three pink dahlias, two bright green leaves, and one bright green reversed leaf.

2. Apply fusible web to the wrong side of the 2"-wide dark green batik strip and cut three ¼" x 17" strips for the stems.

3. Referring to the photo on page 80, arrange the flowers, leaves, and stems on the quilt center, starting with the stems. Trim away the extra length from the stems as needed and tuck the ends under the dark green flange.

4. Once you're satisfied with the placement, fuse the appliqués in place on the quilt top.

Adding the Borders

1. Sew the 2"-wide fabric 7 strips together end to end. From the strip, cut four equal-length strips for the inner border.

2. Repeat step 1 using the 1"-wide dark pink batik strips for the middle border, and then the 4½"-wide fabric 1 strips for the outer border.

3. Sew one inner-border strip, one middle-border strip, and one outer-border strip together along their long sides. Make two side border strips, pressing the seam allowances toward the outer border. Make two border strips for the top and bottom borders and press the seam allowances toward the inner border.

Make 4.

4. Referring to "Borders with Mitered Corners" on page 15, sew the side, and then the top and bottom borders to the quilt top. Press the seam allowances toward the borders. Miter the corners, trim, and then press the seam allowances open.

Finishing the Quilt

1. Measure and cut the backing fabric into two equal lengths; then sew the lengths together using a ½" seam allowance. Trim off the selvages, leaving a ¼" seam allowance. Press the seam allowances open.

2. Layer the quilt top with batting and backing. Baste the layers together.

3. Quilt as desired, or use the quilting suggestions on page 84.

4. Using the 2¼"-wide dark green batik binding strips and referring to "Binding" on page 22, make and attach the binding.

5. If you want to hang your quilt, add a hanging sleeve as described on page 23.

Quilting Suggestions

The flowers were quilted just inside each petal, the leaves were quilted inside the edge, and quilting was used to add veins. The center diamond was stippled and the remaining quilt center and outer border were quilted with swirl-centered flowers. A leafy vine with tendrils was quilted in the inner border and the dark pink border has alternating flower petals and spikes.

Leaf
Pattern is full sized.
Do not enlarge.
Make 2 and 1 reversed.
Pattern pieces do not
include seam allowances.

Dahlia
Pattern is full sized.
Make 3.
Pattern pieces do not
include seam allowances.

Triple Iris

The bearded iris, another of my favorites, is such a regal flower and can be found in some of the most amazing color combinations! If you plant them in a spot they like, they'll grow and multiply with very little care.

Materials

Yardage is based on 42"-wide fabric.

1 yard of tan print for background block, second border, and fifth border

⅞ yard of dark gold batik for first border, fourth border, and binding

⅔ yard of cream print for background block and second border

½ yard of beige batik for background block and third border

¼ yard of black-and-brown floral for corner squares

1 fat quarter (18" x 21") of black batik for vase appliqué

¼ yard of dark green batik for leaf and stem appliqués

¼ yard of gold-and-plum batik for flower appliqués

⅛ yard of medium green 1 batik for leaf appliqués

⅛ yard of medium green 2 batik for leaf appliqués

⅛ yard of apricot batik for flower appliqués

⅛ yard of peach batik for flower appliqués

3" x 3" square of gold batik for flower center appliqués

3 yards of fabric for backing and hanging sleeve*

42" x 42" piece of batting

1¼ yard of 20"-wide fusible web

Freezer paper

Parchment paper

If backing fabric is 42" wide after washing and trimming the selvages, you can use a single width of 1⅝ yards for backing and hanging sleeve.

Cutting

Cut all strips across the width of the fabric.

From the tan print, cut:

* 1 strip, 4⅞" x 42"; crosscut into 4 squares, 4⅞" x 4⅞". Cut each square in half diagonally to yield 8 triangles.
* 2 strips, 4½" x 42"; crosscut into:
  4 rectangles, 4½" x 8½"
  4 squares, 4½" x 4½"
* 4 strips, 2½" x 42"; crosscut into 4 strips, 2½" x 33½"
* 6 strips, 1" x 42"

From the beige batik, cut:

* 2 strips, 1½" x 33½"
* 2 strips, 1½" x 31½"
* 1 square, 8½" x 8½"
* 4 squares, 4½" x 4½"

From the cream print, cut:

* 1 strip, 4½" x 42"; crosscut into 4 rectangles, 4½" x 8½"
* 6 strips, 1" x 42"
* 1 square, 9¼" x 9¼"; cut into quarters diagonally to yield 4 quarter-square triangles

From the dark gold batik, cut:

* 4 strips, 2½" x 42"; crosscut into 4 strips, 2½" x 24½"
* 4 strips, 2¼" x 42"
* 4 strips, 1" x 33½"

From the black-and-brown floral, cut:

* 1 strip, 2½" x 42"; crosscut into 8 squares, 2½" x 2½"
* 4 squares, 2" x 2"

From the dark green batik, cut:

* 1 strip, 2" x 42"

Technique Used

You'll use the following technique when making this quilt.

* Fusible appliqué (page 12)

Making the Background Block

After sewing each seam, press the seam allowances in the direction indicated by the arrows.

1. Lay out one 4½" beige square, one tan square, and one tan rectangle as shown. Sew the squares together, and then sew them to the rectangle to make a corner unit. Make four corner units.

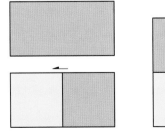

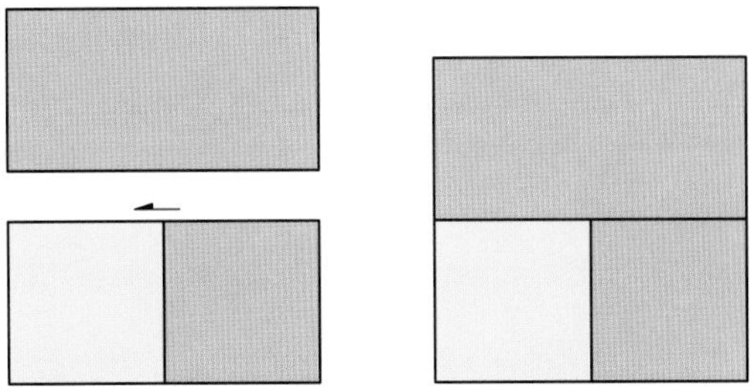

Make 4.

Pieced and quilted by Lynn Ann Majidimehr

Finished quilt: 37½" x 37½"

Finished background block: 24" x 24"

2. Lay out two tan triangles, one cream triangle, and one cream rectangle as shown. Sew the tan triangles to the cream triangle to make a flying-geese unit. Then sew the flying-geese unit to a cream rectangle to make a side unit. Make four side units.

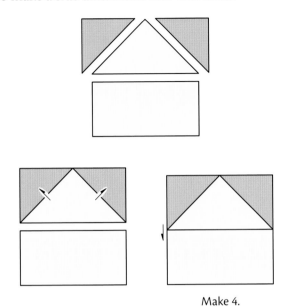

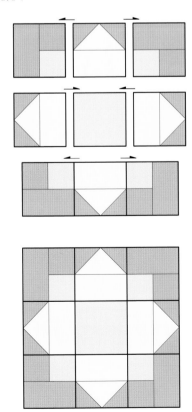

Make 4.

3. Lay out four corner units, four side units, and the 8½" beige square in three rows as shown. Sew the units into rows, and then sew the rows together to complete the block. The block should measure 24½" x 24½".

Making the Striped Border

1. Sew a 1"-wide cream strip and a 1"-wide tan strip together along their long sides to make a strip set. Press the seam allowances toward the tan strip. Make six strip sets.

Make 6.

2. Sew the strip sets from step 1 together in pairs, alternating the cream and tan strips as shown. Press the seam allowances toward the tan strip. Make three of these strip sets. From the strip sets, cut 56 segments, 2" wide.

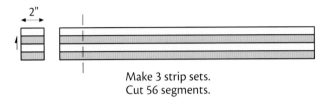

Make 3 strip sets.
Cut 56 segments.

3. Sew 14 segments together to make a border strip as shown in the quilt assembly diagram on page 90. Make four striped border strips.

Adding the Borders

1. Sew 24½"-long dark gold strips to opposite sides of the block and press the seam allowances toward the borders. Sew a 2½" black-and-brown floral square to each end of each remaining 24½"-long dark gold strip. Press the seam allowances toward the strips, and then sew the borders to the top and bottom of the block. The quilt center should measure 28½" x 28½".

2. Sew striped border strips to opposite sides of the quilt top. To continue the striped design around the quilt make sure you position the borders as shown in the quilt diagram. Sew a 2" black-and-brown floral square to each end of each remaining strip. Press the seam allowances toward the strips, and then sew the borders to the top and bottom of the block. The quilt center should measure 31½" x 31½".

3. Sew the 31½"-long beige strips to opposite sides of the quilt top and press the seam allowances toward the borders. Sew the 33½"-long beige strips to the top and bottom of the quilt top; press.

4. For the fourth border, fold the 1"-wide dark gold strips in half lengthwise, *wrong* sides together, and press. Machine baste strips to opposite sides of the quilt top, aligning the raw edges and using a ⅛" seam allowance. Then baste the remaining strips to the top and bottom of the quilt top, overlapping the strips in the corners. Press the border flat to remove any puckers.

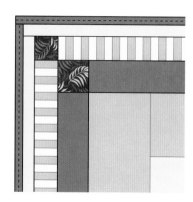

5. Sew 33½"-long tan strips to opposite sides of the quilt top and press the seam allowances toward the borders. Sew a 2½" black-and-brown floral square to each end of each remaining tan strip. Press the seam allowances toward the strips, and then sew the borders to the top and bottom of the quilt top.

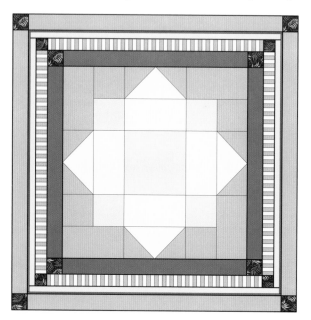

Quilt assembly

Adding the Appliqué

1. Enlarge the patterns on page 92 and use the "Fusible Appliqué" technique to prepare one black batik vase. Using the medium green 1 batik and medium green 2 batik, prepare one curved leaf and 1 reversed curved leaf.

2. Use the patterns on page 91 and the gold-and-plum batik, apricot batik, peach batik, and gold batik to prepare three iris flowers. Use the dark green batik to prepare two spiky leaves and the medium green to prepare one reversed spiky leaf.

3. Apply fusible web to the wrong side of the dark green strip and cut three ¼" x 8" strips for stems.

4. Referring to the photo on page 88, arrange the iris flowers, leaves, and stems on the quilt top, starting with the stems. Position the largest pieces next, and then add the smaller pieces, tucking them underneath the other pieces as needed. Trim away the extra length from the stems as needed.

5. Once you're satisfied with the placement, fuse the appliqués in place on the quilt top.

Finishing the Quilt

1. Measure and cut the backing fabric into two equal lengths; then sew the lengths together using a ½" seam allowance. Trim off the selvages, leaving a ¼" seam allowance. Press the seam allowances open.

2. Layer the quilt top with batting and backing. Baste the layers together.

3. Quilt as desired, or use the quilting suggestions below.

4. Using the 2¼"-wide dark gold binding strips and referring to "Binding" on page 22, make and attach the binding.

5. If you want to hang your quilt, add a hanging sleeve as described on page 23.

 Quilting Suggestions

Heavy contour quilting was used to add shaping to the iris flowers and stems, but the vase was quilted with a simple stipple. Swirls were quilted in the background and fifth border, and a leafy branch was quilted in the dark gold border. The striped and beige borders were quilted with a combination of leaves, curls, and simple swirls.

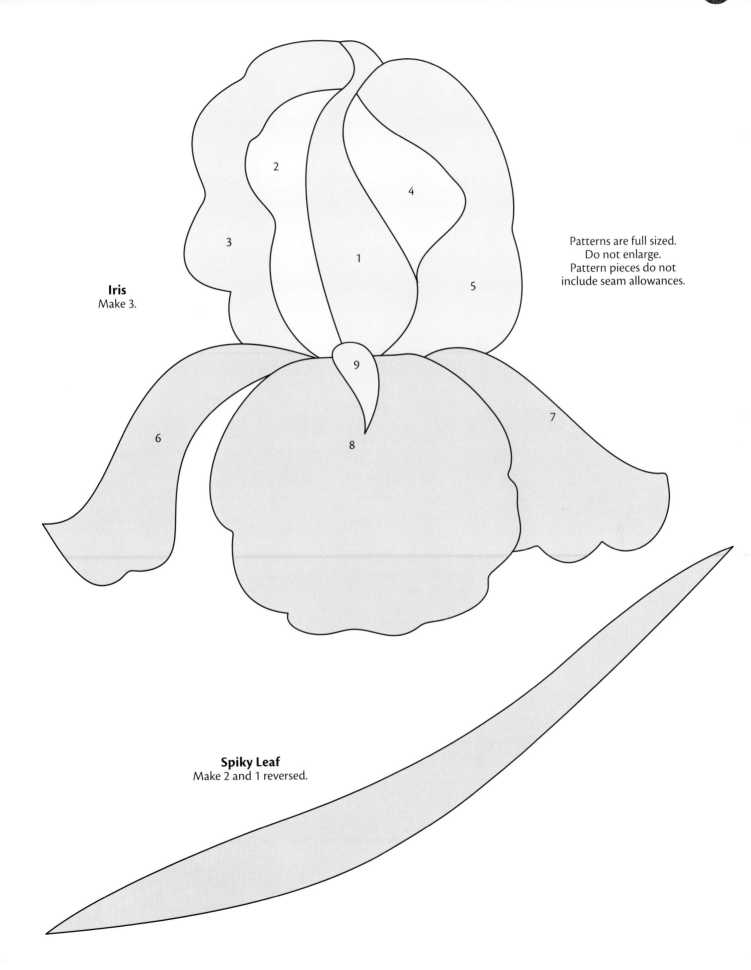

Iris
Make 3.

Patterns are full sized.
Do not enlarge.
Pattern pieces do not
include seam allowances.

Spiky Leaf
Make 2 and 1 reversed.

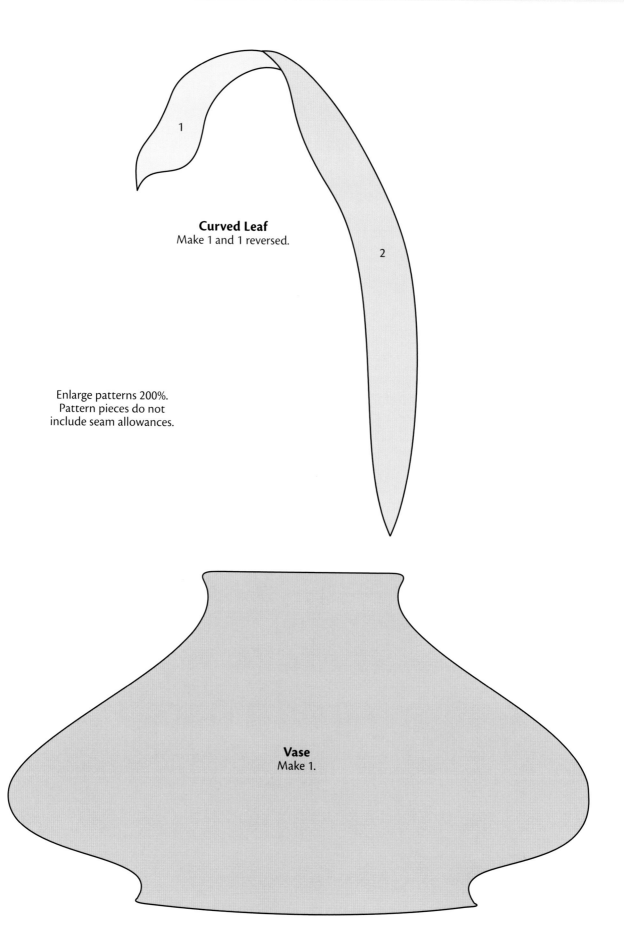

Curved Leaf
Make 1 and 1 reversed.

Enlarge patterns 200%.
Pattern pieces do not
include seam allowances.

Vase
Make 1.

Resources

American Professional Quilting Systems (APQS)
www.apqs.com
Quilting machines

Bernina
www.berninausa.com
Sewing machines and specialty feet

Clever Craft Tools
www.clevercrafttools.com
Quilting disks

eQuilter.com
www.equilter.com
General quilting supplies

Gathering Fabric
www.gatheringfabric.com
General quilting supplies

LAM Designs
http://lynnmajidimehr.com
Patterns from the author, link to her blog, and more

Mistyfuse
www.mistyfuse.com
Ultra-fine, paper-less fusible web

Pfaff
www.pfaffusa.com
Sewing machines and specialty feet

Quiltworks Northwest
www.quiltworksnw.com
General quilting supplies

Superior Threads
www.superiorthreads.com
Sewing and Quilting threads

The Electric Quilt Company
www.electricquilt.com
Quilt-Design Software

YLI Corporation
www.ylicorp.com
YLI Pearl Crown Rayon thread

References

Hand Appliqué by Machine by Beth Ferrier (Applewood Farm Publications, Inc., 2002). Detailed glue basting and machine-appliqué techniques can be found in this book.

Machine Quilting Made Easy! by Maurine Noble (Martingale & Company, 1994). This is my favorite book for teaching machine quilting, and it's the one that helped me make the jump from hand quilting my quilts to machine quilting them.

Machine Quilting with Decorative Threads by Maurine Noble and Elizabeth Hendricks (Martingale & Company, 1998). This book has wonderful tips for using unusual threads, as well as a chart for matching threads and needles, which is very useful.

Mastering the Art of McTavishing by Karen McTavish (On-Word Bound Books, 2005). Karen's free-flowing quilting shapes are wonderful for quilting background areas. Although she's a long-arm quilter, the designs readily translate to home machines, and the CD that comes with this book is invaluable for teaching many different styles.

Threadplay with Libby Lehman by Libby Lehman (Martingale & Company, 1997). Lots of great information on how to set up your machine for different types of stitching, including finishing the edges of fusible appliqués and quilting.

Acknowledgments

A special thank you to Aunt Kay for inspiring me to learn to quilt and for teaching me the basics. Although my grandma told me stories about her mom and auntie quilting, my aunt began quilting with her friends and was the first quilter that I ever knew. Without her, it's probable that I would have never learned to quilt, and this book would not exist.

Thank you to Susan Webster, who likes to say she "discovered me," because she did—thank you for opening your shop so close to our house, encouraging me to share my projects, nudging me to start teaching, urging me to write patterns, and telling me I should write a book! If you hadn't put that bee in my bonnet—along with all your encouragement—this book surely would not exist.

I'd also like to give a big thank you to the Martingale & Company staff. Working with Cathy, Karen, and Nancy has been a wonderful learning experience, and yet I know there were many others behind the scenes that helped make this book possible. Thank you!

About the Author

Photo taken by Amir Majidimehr

Lynn Majidimehr is a mixed-media textile artist who has sewn and been interested in art since she was young. Because she grew up with a mom, aunt, and grandmother who sewed, it was natural for Lynn to learn how to sew too. By high school, she could already sew garments and embroider, but it was her aunt who started her on a quilting journey. Her early quilts were traditional and hand quilted, because that was how she was taught, but Lynn has migrated toward more contemporary, sometimes bright quilts, which are machine quilted. Most of her creative time is spent making textile art and quilts, although she also enjoys working in many other media. Some of her more recent quilts are a fusion of quilting and painting, where the design comes alive when they're combined.

She has lived on both East and West Coasts, and now calls Washington state her home. Until Gathering Fabric Quilt Shop opened just down the hill from her home, she hadn't really shown her quilts to many people, other than family and friends. The shop's owner, Susan Webster, was just setting up shop when she and Lynn met, and soon Lynn was teaching at the shop. Lynn designed a shop-hop block, was urged to create a pattern, and before she knew it, LAM Designs was born. It all started with that first pattern and has continued to grow.

Lynn has had quilts shown in the 2008 Pacific Northwest Quiltfest, 2008 Quilts: A World of Beauty, and 2009 Innovations Quilt Show, as well as local shows. Her Harvest Gathering Quilt Pattern was first published in the 2004 Premier Fall Issue of *Quilt Sampler* magazine.

There's More Online!

* Find quilts, patterns, class information, and more at www.lynnmajidimehr.com.

* Discover more great quilting and craft books at www.martingale-pub.com.

You might also enjoy these other fine titles from

Martingale & Company

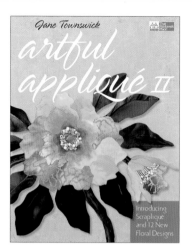

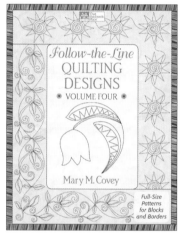

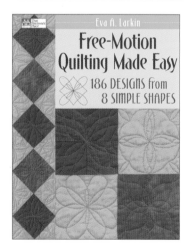

Our books are available at bookstores and your favorite craft, fabric, and yarn retailers.
Visit us at www.martingale-pub.com or contact us at:

That Patchwork Place®

America's Best-Loved Quilt Books®

Martingale®
& COMPANY

America's Best-Loved Craft & Hobby Books®
America's Best-Loved Knitting Books®

1-800-426-3126
International: 1-425-483-3313
Fax: 1-425-486-7596
Email: info@martingale-pub.com